DATE DUE

DEC 13

ALEXANDER HAMILTON

Not many people have devoted themselves so diligently to the welfare of the United States as did Alexander Hamilton. As a boy he was always advanced in manner, vocabulary and intelligence. At the age of twelve, he began a successful career working for a trading firm, and at nineteen he was appointed captain of an artillery company. Here in detail is the story of Hamilton's life, from his birth on an island in the West Indies to the eventful day in Weehawken, New Jersey, when he was fatally wounded in a duel with Aaron Burr. Many of us do not realize the influence Alexander Hamilton had on the "young" United States and some of us do not feel that he was completely justified in many of his causes, but most of us respect him as a man who loved his country and who was willing to work and fight to make it a better place in which to live.

ALEXANDER HAMILTON

ALEXANDER HAMILTON

By

WILLIAM WISE

G. P. PUTNAM'S SONS

NEW YORK

CONTENTS

To Nina and Alfred

ALEXANDER HAMILTON

1

ON NEVIS AND ST. CROIX

If you happen to walk down a certain out-of-the-way street in New York City, just a block or two from upper Broadway, you will find a curious, old-fashioned wooden house that has fallen into ruin. It is called "The Grange." The front steps are broken, the paint has peeled away, and whenever it rains the roof leaks and the house must be closed to visitors.

The Grange, an almost forgotten museum now, was once the home of Alexander Hamilton, who built it more than a hundred and sixty years ago. Here, Hamilton settled with his family, hopeful of enjoying a quiet middle-age. Here, two years later, he made his will, and wrote a farewell letter to his wife. And here, early one summer morning, he walked down the front steps, mounted his horse, and rode off to fight a duel with Aaron Burr.

The owner of The Grange did not return. Soon, the shutters of the house were closed. And closed as well was the last chapter in the life of a great and controversial American.

* * *

A half century before, in 1753, Alexander Hamilton's father, James Hamilton, an aristocratic but almost penniless Scotsman, came to the West Indies to make his fortune. He met Rachel Fawcett, and they fell in love, but Rachel was not free to marry him. Her family had forced her, at sixteen, to marry a wealthy middle-aged Danish planter named John Levine. Levine had been a cruel husband and Rachel soon left him, but when she met James Hamilton she was still Levine's wife.

Though she tried for several years, Rachel could not obtain a divorce. Finally, when she was twenty, she gave James what money she had, so that he could set himself up as a trader. And then she sailed with him to the British island of Nevis, where she owned a small house, and became his common-law wife. Alexander Hamilton was born on Nevis the following year, on the 11th of January, 1757.

He was a healthy, active child who loved the out-of-doors. He was also surprisingly precocious. When he was three, he insisted that his mother teach him to read and write. At four, he learned to recite the Ten Commandments in Hebrew; the task only took him a few days.

When Alexander was five, his mother had another child, James, named after the boys' father. Scarcely had the baby arrived when the elder James announced that he had failed in business. He had lost all of Rachel's money, and since he had no money of his own, he and his family were practically paupers.

The house on Nevis was sold, and Alexander, his infant brother, and their parents sailed to the neighboring island of St. Croix. They moved into a small white house on the crest of a hill. The house was part of a sugar plantation that belonged to Peter Lytton, the husband of one of Rachel's two married sisters. Peter Lytton had agreed to hire James Hamilton as his overseer. But for the aristocratic James, who had never worked for anyone else, this was a humiliating comedown.

There were times when life on Peter Lytton's remote sugar plantation seemed lonely to Alexander. He had no companions his own age and there was no school for him to attend. Fortunately, he loved to read, and his mother, when she had finished her household chores, enjoyed talking and reading with him.

Then, on his sixth birthday, his father gave him a pony, and after that, whenever he wasn't busy with his books, he was out riding through the fields of sugar cane or along the dusty road that ran past the plantation. Sometimes he explored the hills that rose behind the house, sometimes he roamed the steep valleys that cut between them; when it was hot, he swam in the mountain streams, and when it was cooler, he hunted small game and land crabs and wild birds.

One evening his father returned from Christiansted, the capital of St. Croix, bringing with him a guest, a young Presbyterian minister named Hugh Knox. The minister was a well-educated man. He owned a large library—large, at least, by the standards of the West Indies planters and merchants, whose great homes around Christiansted usually had more copper pots in the kitchen than books in the parlor.

Hugh Knox became a regular visitor at the lonely plantation. From the very first he was astonished by Alexander. It seemed impossible to believe that a mere six-year-old boy could possess such an active and mature mind. He offered to become Alexander's teacher. He told Rachel what she had long believed herself, that her son's natural intelligence was remarkable, and that he undoubtedly had a brilliant future ahead of him. A famous poet—that's what Hugh Knox was sure he would become.

During the next two years, the minister brought many of

his own books to the plantation for Alexander to read. He was a kindly man, and he became the boy's friend and adviser, as well as the earliest and strongest of his admirers. According to Hugh Knox there was little that Alexander couldn't hope to accomplish if only he continued to apply himself to his studies.

After three years on St. Croix, Alexander's mother heard some disturbing news. Peter Lytton was thoroughly dissatisfied with the way James Hamilton was running the plantation. James was too impetuous. He made decisions too quickly, and those decisions invariably cost Peter Lytton a good deal of money.

Soon matters grew even worse. There were several sharp quarrels between James and his employer, and then, another costly mistake. Peter Lytton spoke angrily, insultingly, and James, his pride hurt beyond endurance, declared that he was resigning a position which he was allowed to hold only because of Rachel and her children.

James, however, assured Rachel that the future still looked bright. He said he was going to sail to the distant island of St. Vincent, where he would be able to make a fresh start. He would find work with some traders he knew there, and as soon as he was back on his feet again he would send for Rachel and their two sons.

James Hamilton was gone from St. Croix on the next ship that sailed away to the south. Rachel, Alexander and little James moved from the plantation. They went to live in Peter Lytton's great house, just outside Christiansted. They were now entirely dependent on Peter Lytton's charity.

Alexander was eight, old enough to be shocked at his father's desertion, and observant enough to detect any change in his mother's manner or appearance. In time, he noticed that her cheeks grew rosy and her eyes brightened only when

someone arrived at her rooms carrying a letter from the latest
ship to reach Christiansted from St. Vincent. He also noticed
that her cheeks soon lost their color and her eyes soon grew
dull again as she read the letter—and how, as the months went
by, those letters became fewer and fewer.

If Alexander hadn't realized how unhappy his mother was,
and if he hadn't missed his father, he would have been completely pleased with his new life in Peter Lytton's house. He
was no longer without friends. Several boys, the sons of the
leading English planters on St. Croix, lived on the neighboring estates. Alexander, Benjamin Yard, Thomas and Edward
Stevens, all rode horseback together, and played games, and
studied with Hugh Knox.

Alexander's best friend was Edward Stevens, a distant
cousin. "Neddy" Stevens, like the other boys, soon came to
accept Alexander as their leader, even though he was younger
than the rest of them and very much smaller. They instinctively admired his enthusiasm, his imagination, and his fear-
lessness, and were willing to obey his commands and to
undertake whatever strenuous adventures he planned for
them.

Once in a while Alexander lost his temper, for he had a
fiery one, and then there would be a terrific fistfight behind
Peter Lytton's barn. But most of the time he was good-
humored and generous, and the other boys never seemed to
hold these rare outbursts against him.

Sometimes they played soldier. Alexander was their captain.
He marched them up and down King Street in the tropical
sun for half the morning, but they put up with their tiny
martinet because they saw that no matter how much he asked
of them, he invariably asked twice as much of himself.

Alexander enjoyed his schooling with Hugh Knox. He
studied Latin, Greek, chemistry, mathematics and French.
The last was an invaluable asset in the West Indies, because

so many of the island merchants and government officials were either French themselves, or spoke and wrote French as their second language.

Hugh Knox continued to be Alexander's leading partisan. He never missed a chance to praise the hard work and talent of his pupil, especially to Alexander's wealthy aunts and uncles, to Peter and Mary Lytton, and to Thomas Mitchell, a leading merchant on St. Croix, and to Ann Mitchell, his wife.

Alexander's relatives told Hugh Knox that they were pleased to hear how "talented" their unfortunate nephew was. They hoped that because of his intelligence he would not come to grief in the world as his ill-starred father had. But only Ann Mitchell really believed that his gifts were as extraordinary as the minister claimed.

By now, three years had passed in Peter Lytton's house. Alexander was no longer the only one who noticed the slow, awful change in his mother. She was never gay or lighthearted any more, she rarely smiled, her eyes were weary, somber, remote.

The letters from St. Vincent had almost stopped. For a year James had not even mentioned the possibility of Rachel and the children joining him. And as hopeless month followed hopeless month, she finally had to admit to herself that the man she loved, the man she had given her money to, the father of her children, no longer loved her in return.

Her heart broke, and in a few weeks, on the 25th of February, 1768, when she was thirty-two, Rachel died. She was buried in the Lyttons' private burial ground across the valley.

Alexander was eleven, his brother James was six. With no parents to protect them, or to provide for their welfare, they were now little better than orphans.

2

CRUGER & COMPANY

AFTER their mother's death, Alexander and his brother James never saw very much of each other again. Alexander went to live with Thomas and Ann Mitchell, while James returned to Peter Lytton's house, where he lived for a number of years, until he was old enough to be apprenticed to a local carpenter.

James had none of Alexander's natural gifts, none of his physical or mental vigor, none of his curiosity or ambition. The two brothers were so different in mind and temperament that they had never been friends. When their lives turned in separate directions they parted easily and without regret.

At the Mitchells', Alexander was allowed for a brief time to continue his studies. Then his two uncles discussed the matter and decided that since Alexander would have to earn his living sooner or later anyway, he might as well begin at once.

Ann Mitchell protested but she was overruled. Hugh Knox tried to convince Thomas Mitchell and Peter Lytton that

their extraordinary nephew should receive a higher education, a year or two of further study on St. Croix, and then
several years at college in the American Colonies or in Europe.
Alexander's uncles said that they were willing to support
their nephew while he served an apprenticeship on St. Croix.
That, and no more, was what they were willing to do for him.

And so, when he was twelve years old, Alexander had to
give up his regular schooling and go to work, leaving behind
at their desks his more fortunate friends and classmates.

He soon decided that he did not want to work for either
of his uncles. Peter Lytton was kindly enough, but the only
position he could offer was an unskilled job on one of his
remote sugar plantations, a job with no real prospects for the
future. In Thomas Mitchell's counting house there might be
a better chance of advancement, but Thomas Mitchell was
surly and short-tempered, especially when he was suffering
from the gout.

Put us together, Alexander thought, and we'd fight every
day. No, Uncle Thomas and I would not get along.

In Christiansted there was a firm of merchants called Nicholas Cruger & Company. Arrangements were made for Alexander to talk with the senior partner about becoming his
apprenticed clerk. One morning he walked down Strand
Street, stopped in front of a white rambling building that
faced the harbor, and entered Nicholas Cruger's office.

When he told Mr. Cruger who he was, the merchant opened
his eyes a little. He stared at Alexander. The boy in front of
him was short, his body was thin. He looked like a child of
nine or ten, and not a very robust or healthy child.

"So *you're* Alexander Hamilton," Nicholas Cruger finally
said. "I thought you'd be bigger."

"My size, sir," Alexander said, looking straight into Mr.

Cruger's large, red face, "will not affect the amount of work I do."

Mr. Cruger saw that despite appearances he was not dealing with an ordinary ten- or twelve-year-old. He coughed, to hide his surprise. "And you think you can learn enough to become one of my clerks?"

"I'm sure that I can, sir."

The merchant shook his head doubtfully. "Well, it's true that your uncle, Peter Lytton, is no fool, and he did speak highly of you the other day. But of course you *are* his nephew, so his opinion doesn't count for much, does it?"

Alexander said nothing. It seemed an excellent time to keep still.

"I *do* know Hugh Knox's judgment can be trusted," Nicholas Cruger continued. "Dr. Knox tells me that you're the best student he's ever had. A real prodigy. Well—are you?"

"That would hardly be for *me* to say," Alexander replied.

"True, perfectly true," Mr. Cruger said. "All right, suppose I should tell you that you can have a try at it? When could you start to work for me?"

"I can start now," Alexander said.

He saw Nicholas Cruger smile. "That's a businesslike answer. Very well, let's say that your application has been accepted. I'll show you the desk where you'll work. And we'll see soon enough if you're cut out to be a clerk in my counting house."

It was not long before Nicholas Cruger's doubts were dissolved. His new apprentice learned quickly, and what he had once learned he never forgot. In a few months Alexander had become a useful member of the firm and was promoted from apprentice to regular clerk.

As a result, he began to receive a salary. Though he continued to live in Thomas Mitchell's winter home in Christiansted so that he would not have to pay rent, he did begin to pay for his clothing and for his other personal expenses. He felt a great satisfaction on the day when he received his salary for the first time, and knew that in the eyes of Thomas Mitchell and Peter Lytton he was no longer a small but irritating burden.

The operations of Cruger & Company were many and varied. Nicholas Cruger had lived for many years in New York City. The company still maintained a business office there which was run by some of the other partners. The company owned a warehouse in New York, private docks there to unload its ships, and a distillery to convert molasses into rum.

The company also had banking and trading interests in such remote and exotic places as Honduras, Jamaica and Curaçao, and in Bristol, England. Cruger & Company sailed their own ships and loaned money to other traders and merchants. The company financed merchants who were in the slave trade, one of the most profitable and surely one of the most shameful business enterprises of that era—and one in which many "respectable" and "honorable" men took part.

As time went by, Alexander became increasingly familiar with the price and the quality, the origin and the ultimate destination of dozens and dozens of different types of goods. There was West Indian sugar, molasses and mahogany, which the ships of Cruger & Company carried to the American Colonies; there were horses, mules, flour, dried and salted meats and fish, which the same ships carried back from America to the Islands. There were manufactured goods, iron and copperware, silks, glass and china, which came to the Islands from England; there were hides, tobacco, furs, rice and sugar, the raw wealth of the western world, which returned to England.

And at the center of all this commercial activity was the counting house of Nicholas Cruger & Company. Seated before his desk on a high stool, his quill bobbing up and down, Alexander worked and listened and learned. He copied invoices and bills of lading, balanced accounts, and made duplicates of the letters which Mr. Cruger wrote to other traders and to the company's many captains, whose ships were scattered over half of the Western Hemisphere. In later years, both Alexander's political allies and his political foes were astonished at his grasp of financial matters. Economic theories he learned from books. Practical knowledge came from his experience at Cruger & Company when he was a boy just entering his teens.

Nicholas Cruger was pleased with the work of his industrious but frail-looking young clerk. If he thought about it at all, he assumed that Alexander was equally pleased to be working in the counting house, learning the business.

Nothing could have been further from the truth. The boy who had loved to play soldier, who had loved to plan exciting adventures for himself and his friends, found the life of a lowly clerk boresome. He missed the hours spent out-of-doors, when he had hunted and swam, and had ridden a horse through the woods and valleys of the island. He missed the pleasure of his daily lessons with Hugh Knox. He missed the companionship of his more fortunate friends, who were still going to school, still riding and hunting in their leisure hours, still living the pleasant life of young English gentlemen, a life which he had shared with them only a few months before.

At Cruger & Company Alexander finally understood just how much he had been hurt by his father's failures. Because of them, he was now poor, and with a very modest education. His future prospects were dim. They depended entirely on his own efforts. Unless he was extremely lucky, he seemed destined to spend the rest of his youth in the rambling white building that overlooked the harbor of Christiansted. Perhaps he would spend his entire life there.

And yet, he refused to believe it. He refused to believe that he was destined to be no more than a mere drudge in Nicholas Cruger's counting house. He looked at the other clerks, poor, drab, spiritless creatures, content to live from day to day in the easy, indolent way of the tropics, achieving nothing, aspiring to nothing, hoping for nothing—and he pitied them heartily.

The world, he thought, was too beautiful, too challenging, too vast and exciting a place for any man of spirit to be content with such a fate.

Obstinately, passionately, he began to tell himself that a more satisfying destiny awaited him somewhere else. He didn't know where it might await him. Perhaps in England, in Europe, in the American Colonies. He had no idea what that destiny might be. But surely, with the God-given intelligence that he knew had been bestowed on him, and with the vitality and ambition that he felt burning in his body and in his brain, he couldn't believe that he was meant to waste himself forever in the sleepy, provincial town of Christiansted.

He began to imagine different ways of escaping from the prison of Cruger & Company, of the brave and astonishing deeds he would subsequently perform, and of the great fame that would be his at last. And with that fame, he would restore his family's honor, would redeem his father's failures, and would avenge his mother for the snubs and insults she had once received from a few of the "better" people on Nevis and St. Croix.

Particularly he dreamed of smoky, bloodstained battlefields, where heroes were made through their own valor and daring, and where nobody could ask a man—with a hidden sneer—just who his mother and father were or what their exact position had been in society.

But while he indulged his imagination in the most heroic and romantic visions, Alexander rarely forgot the practical

side of his daily life. Before daydreaming, he finished his
work. He finished it promptly and faultlessly. Only then did
he put down his pen for a minute or two and gaze through
the window at the harbor and the sea—the sea that he hoped
to cross one day on his way to fame and fortune.

3

THE FIRST COMMAND

THERE was another dream that Alexander cherished secretly while he continued to work in the counting house at Cruger & Company. It was the dream of completing his formal education. He knew that an ignorant man, poor and without strong family connections, had little chance of a successful career, and he knew himself to be lamentably ignorant by the standards of well-educated people in Europe or in the large eastern cities of North America.

So he continued his schoolwork and his reading, in the hope that one day he might go to college and perhaps be able to enter medicine or the law. After working all day at the counting house he sat up far into the night with books that his friend, Hugh Knox, loaned him. During his early teens Alexander's reading included Plutarch, Plato, Shakespeare, Milton, Pope, and other Greek philosophers and English poets; he also read several abridged histories of England and Europe.

One evening as he was leaving work Alexander met his

friend Ned Stevens. Neddy was bubbling over with excitement. He told "Ham"—Ham was Alexander's nickname—that in a few days he was going to sail to New York, to enter Kings College.

Alexander congratulated his friend on his good fortune; he was genuinely happy that Neddy Stevens was so lucky. But this did not seem greatly to ease his feelings of anger and frustration over the fact that he himself, being without a father's assistance, was unable to go to college too.

As soon as he could he rushed away to Hugh Knox's house, where he found the minister in his study.

"Of course it's unfair," Hugh Knox said, after he had listened to Alexander's outburst. "You're a better student than Ned. Why, Neddy himself would be the first to admit that. But many things in the world aren't fair, and we must learn to accept our disappointments with good grace."

"But I'm *tired* of accepting things with good grace!" Alexander said. "I've always wanted to go to college. I've studied harder than anyone else. And I know I'll never go. Never."

"And I say that one day you will," Hugh Knox said. "Sooner or later the money will be raised. I've been talking with your uncles again. Tom Mitchell is hopeless, that much I'll admit. But there's hope in Peter Lytton. I'm sure that eventually he'll change his mind and agree to help you. I mean to keep after him. And you, Ham—you must learn patience."

Alexander continued to study at night and to work during the day at the counting house. He did his best to remain cheerful and patient, but sometimes even Hugh Knox's optimism failed to reassure his doubts about the future and then he fell into a mood of despair.

In a letter written during the unhappy days at Cruger & Company, he talked of his ambition, his discontent and his vague but persistent plans for the future. The letter was written on the 11th of November, 1769, to Ned Stevens, soon after the latter had reached New York.

Alexander wrote to his friend, ". . . to confess my weakness, Ned, my ambition is so prevalent that I [scorn] the groveling condition of a clerk, to which my fortune, etc., condemns me, and would willingly risk my life, though not my character, to exalt my station. I am confident, Ned, that my youth excludes me from any hope of immediate preferment; . . . but I mean to prepare the way for futurity. I . . . may be justly said to build castles in the air; my folly makes me ashamed, and I beg you conceal it; yet, Neddy, we have seen such schemes successful when the projector is constant. I shall conclude by saying I wish there was a war."

But there was no war to which Alexander could escape, and so he was forced to remain at his desk, his expression cheerful but his heart heavy with discontent.

As the months passed, Nicholas Cruger's respect for Alexander's intelligence, judgment and good sense continued to grow. He decided to reward his young clerk by sending him off alone to the town of Frederiksted, on the eastern side of the island, to be in sole charge of the company's branch office there. It was an unusual indication of the senior partner's trust and confidence in him, and at first Alexander was both pleased and flattered. But after a few days in Frederiksted he began to wish that Nicholas Cruger had chosen someone else for the position of trust.

Never before had he appreciated the beauties and comforts of Christiansted, the capital. Frederiksted was small, hot and ugly. Nothing ever happened in the town. When he finished his work at the office he had no one to talk with and nowhere to go. After supper each night he returned to his room, drew out one of the books he had brought with him, and with a sigh, settled down to another evening of study and solitude.

For six months, night after night, he read Shakespeare and Pope and Plato at the desk in his dark, stifling room. He read by the light of two candles. Mosquitoes bit him unceasingly; cockroaches, some as long as his hand, crawled across the desk; an occasional land crab wandered into the room and rattled over the floor; a poisonous centipede, exhibiting an unusual interest in literature, appeared without warning on the page of his book.

One morning there was a message in the office, summoning him back to Christiansted. After an exile of six months, Alexander flung his few linen shirts into a bag and left as quickly as he could. When he reached the capital, it seemed like an earthly paradise.

Then, in the autumn of 1771, Nicholas Cruger fell seriously ill. At first he consulted a local doctor, but his health failed to improve. He decided to go to New York for further treatment.

A week before he was to sail he called Alexander to his office. He told Alexander that he had decided to appoint him chief clerk at Cruger & Company, and that during his own absence, which would last at least several months, Alexander was to be in complete charge of the business.

When the news came out, people said that Nicholas Cruger had taken leave of his wits. Rival merchants insisted that to place a mere boy, not quite fifteen years old, in a position of such authority was to court financial disaster.

Nicholas Cruger remained unperturbed. Alexander already knew the procedures of trade quite thoroughly. He was hardworking, his judgment was sound, he was remarkably mature for his age. The senior partner confidently sailed for New York on the 15th of October, 1771, and Alexander took command.

His days at Cruger & Company were far different now from

what they had been before. Instead of merely copying Mr. Cruger's letters, he wrote all the letters himself. Instead of copying bills of lading, he inspected the cargoes. He bartered and bargained, he sent full instructions to the company's captains, he loaned money to other merchants, and all the while he kept a stream of reports flowing to Nicholas Cruger in New York.

Every third or fourth day, off went another letter. He spoke of good and bad bargains, he spoke of other traders who had dealt unfairly, he spoke of shipments which had arrived in poor condition.

Very little escaped his sharp eye. "Your Philadelphia flour," he wrote to Nicholas Cruger on one occasion, "is really very bad . . . the bakers complain that they cannot by any means get it to rise. . . . Upon opening several barrels I have observed a kind of Worm, very common in flour, about the surface—which is an indication of Age—it could not have been very new when it was shipped."

Being in charge of Cruger & Company was a marvelous opportunity for Alexander. In a few months he had learned every facet of the complex trading and banking business. He also had learned to work long hours under constant pressure, he had become accustomed to directing others who were older than himself, and most important of all, he had formed the habit of making rapid and responsible decisions under circumstances of confusion and uncertainty. He had never felt so happy in his work. The counting house no longer seemed a prison. Christiansted no longer seemed a hopeless provincial town, to be escaped at the first opportunity.

After a few weeks Alexander's health, which was never really strong, finally broke down. It would break down again and again in later years, whenever he placed too great a strain on his frail constitution. But now, characteristically, he was too proud to leave his post. He wrote to Nicholas Cruger, "I am so unwell that it is with difficulty I make out to write these few lines. . . . I have sold about 30 barrels of flour more and collected a little more money from different people." Then he returned to his room and fought against the fever until he had conquered it.

In New York, Nicholas Cruger recovered his health quite rapidly. Late in March, 1772, after an absence of a little more than six months, the senior partner returned to St. Croix.

He found his business flourishing, and he congratulated Alexander with great enthusiasm and affection. He also found that his chief clerk had changed. Though only a lad of fifteen, Alexander now possessed the self-assurance and the presence of mind that would have done credit to a man twice his age.

One evening, not long after Nicholas Cruger's return, Alexander sat alone in his room and thought about his future. Mr. Cruger had talked with him that day, and had hinted that in a year or two he intended to offer Alexander a junior partnership in the firm. A commercial career, public esteem, a high position in local society, would all be his. He would eventually be prosperous enough to buy one of the great houses outside the town, and would walk on terms of equality with anyone from Nevis, St. Christopher or St. Croix.

It would mean, of course, that he would never leave the Islands for long, and would never perform any of the heroic deeds that he had once imagined. He would never go to college either. But his hopes of escaping from St. Croix, of going to college, had already faded. He and Hugh Knox still talked about the money that Peter Lytton might be persuaded to part with one day—just as they had talked about it two years before.

If he was not to have fame, if he was not to perform great deeds of valor, if he was not to go to college and enter medicine or the law—then perhaps he had stumbled into the next best thing. A partnership in Cruger & Company—it wouldn't be too bad an achievement, he thought, for a penniless boy, forced to make his own way in the world.

Now in every man's life there are times when Chance enters unexpectedly; some totally unlooked-for event takes place, and afterwards he finds that his prospects, his hopes, his entire future have changed, and will never be the same again.

Such an event took place on St. Croix, early in the autumn of 1772. A great hurricane, the most severe in a hundred years, began to approach the island. If the storm had passed a few hundred miles to the north or a few hundred miles to the south, Alexander Hamilton's life would have been vastly different. And the history of the United States might have been vastly different, too.

4

THE HURRICANE

ALEXANDER was in the counting house at Cruger & Company when he heard the first dull, low roar of the wind out of the southeast. He and Mr. Cruger consulted a barometer, and Mr. Cruger rubbed his red face and frowned. The reading was ominously low. A half hour later, when they looked again, the barometer had fallen almost another half point.

"I think," Mr. Cruger said, "that we're going to be hit head on. And by a very severe storm."

As though in answer, the guns began to boom in the fort that guarded the harbor in Christiansted. They had never been used within anyone's memory. They were only used to signal disaster; their sound meant that the island now stood directly in the hurricane's path.

As soon as they heard the guns Mr. Cruger and Alexander separated, Mr. Cruger to secure the building and his own house against the storm, Alexander to alert his relatives, Peter Lytton and Ann Mitchell, and to do what he could to help them.

When he came out of the counting house, Alexander was almost flung bodily across Strand Street. The wind was howling, shingles were flying through the air, salt spray from the harbor was falling in the street.

Alexander ran to the Mitchells' winter house. He saw that the solid wooden hurricane windows were already bolted in place. Thomas Mitchell was away on a trading voyage and Ann was living alone on their plantation, beyond Peter Lytton's house.

Alexander saddled a horse in Thomas Mitchell's barn and led the horse outside. He had to lead it around the corner, out of the wind, before he could mount it. Strong as the horse was, it staggered uncertainly when the force of the wind first struck it. Around the corner, Alexander was finally able to scramble into the saddle and ride away.

He set out for the Lyttons' plantation. Luckily he was an expert horseman. Even so, he had never been on such a ride in his life. The wind was still rising. It bent the tall royal palms along the main highway that ran from Christiansted to Frederiksted; it shook the seeds that hung by the millions in their dry pods on the "shaggy-shaggy" trees, and the sound they made was exactly like the sound of hailstones hammering on a metal roof.

Alexander saw other riders streaking across the countryside to alert distant plantations to the danger; he saw trees bend and break, and thatched roofs, branches, a door, a small cart, pieces of furniture, sail wildly through the air, sometimes missing his horse, sometimes missing his own head, by only a foot or two.

He knew that his life was in danger, out in the open. But instead of fear, he felt a tremendous sense of exultation, a wild excitement as the wind roared and the rain began to pour down out of the gray, menacing clouds.

He arrived at Peter Lytton's plantation at a gallop and

tethered his horse behind the barn. To reach the house he had to crawl on his hands and knees across the open court-yard, for it was impossible to walk upright in the face of the wind.

The building was barricaded, the hurricane windows were in place; all measures had been taken to secure the main house against the force of the storm. His uncle urged him to stay. He might easily meet with an accident if he rode on. But when Alexander reminded him that Ann Mitchell was alone with her slaves on the Mitchell plantation, Peter Lytton agreed that he should go there.

Alexander passed through one other estate before he came to the Mitchells' property. He rode through the cane fields, clinging to the horse's mane, his body pressed low against the animal's neck. By now he was soaking wet, his shirt had been torn to ribbons, his long hair was streaming and wild.

Ann Mitchell was trying to secure one of the hurricane windows when he came into the living room of the main house. The slaves were crouched in the cellar, too frightened to do anything but pray. Alexander ran to his aunt's side. Without a word of greeting they flung themselves against the window, and with a burst of strength, rammed the heavy metal bolts into place.

For the rest of the day and most of the night, Alexander and his aunt battled to save the house from destruction. Ann Mitchell's hair was unpinned, the sleeve of her gown was torn, her lace cap had been flung aside on a table. Alexander was soaked with rain and sweat, but there was no time to bathe and to change into some of his uncle's dry clothes.

Outside, all was bedlam. The wind howled, the rain pelted down in a flood, trees were blown over and came crashing to earth, shaking the ground, the windows, the furniture. For a time the house was unharmed. Then a tree not far away was uprooted. It fell, smashing into a corner of the roof. The noise, the shudder that went through the walls, was terrible. Below in the cellar, frightened by the din, the slaves set up a loud cry.

Alexander sped up to the attic. The rain was pouring in through a hole in the roof. With water streaming into his eyes he seized a hammer and managed to nail a thick piece of board against the inner side of the roof. Even in a few minutes the heavy downpour had soaked the attic floor, and the wind, funneling in through the hole, had scattered boxes and packing crates as though they were made of paper.

When the eye of the hurricane passed over them, Alexander and his aunt ate some bananas in the kitchen. There was nothing else in the house to eat, and no time to prepare anything. Soon the lull was over. The wind swung around, blowing this time from the west. The storm rose even higher; it blew against the doors, the windows, the walls, as if it meant to rip the house from its foundations and blow it to pieces. The rain fell harder. From the cellar came the sounds of the slaves praying and moaning. Along the beams in the kitchen a stream of terrified rats raced back and forth, almost mad with fright.

All at once in the living room there was the sound of a metal bolt snapping, and one of the heavy hurricane windows blew in. The wind tore through the room, and in a few seconds, half of the furniture was driven against the opposite wall.

For three hours Alexander and his aunt held the hurricane window shut and the bolt in place, straining their arms until their muscles screamed with pain and there seemed to be no breath left in their aching lungs.

And then, slowly, the worst of the hurricane began to pass. As the first faint traces of daylight appeared beyond the windows, as the wind fell and the rain lost its fury, Alexander and his aunt relaxed their struggle. Too exhausted to walk upstairs to bed, they stretched out on the living room furniture and fell asleep.

5

THE "HURRICANE LETTER"

Two days later, having helped Ann Mitchell repair her house, Alexander rode back toward Christiansted. The cane fields were in ruins. The crops lay torn and battered on the soggy ground. The great plantation houses had survived, but many of their barns had been blown down, along with the thatched huts of the slaves. Here and there the wall of a hut still remained standing. In the wreckage, among the debris, a few homeless slaves slowly hunted for their possessions—a battered stool, a cooking pot, a kitchen ladle.

Destruction and death were everywhere. Along the main highway nothing remained of the magnificent royal palms except their long, gray, headless trunks. In the fields, snakes and lizards sunned themselves on the upturned roots of a dead tree which had been flung there, a hundred feet from the highway, by the force of the wind. Mills and distilleries were destroyed. Huge tanks of molasses had burst and the liquid had poured out on the ground, where it lay rotten and stinking. Dead cattle lay in the fields, and under the walls of the fallen buildings there were the bodies of men.

Approaching the capital there were fewer marks of destruction. The houses, because they stood closer together, had acted to protect each other, and only a few houses had lost their roofs and had been flooded by the rain.

But the trees were uprooted on all sides, the lovely flower gardens were piled high with dead plants and rubbish, and down near the harbor, in the park behind the fort, there were many wrecked ships. They had been left high and dry with their sides or their bottoms staved in. Among them were masses of decaying fish, blown ashore by the storm.

Alexander discovered that Thomas Mitchell's house was unharmed. Then he rode over to Company Street to see what had happened to Hugh Knox and his recent bride. The minister, pale and weary, was sitting in his study, about to strengthen his nerves with a glass of sugared rum.

Hugh Knox told Alexander what the hurricane had been like in Christiansted, and then he asked what Alexander had seen and done since leaving the town.

Alexander's mind was still filled with the excitement of the storm, his wild ride to Ann Mitchell's plantation, and the struggle there to save the house. Forgetting himself completely, he poured out the story while Hugh Knox listened, utterly spellbound.

When Alexander had finished, the minister said, "You must write it down. All of it. Today. While your memory's still fresh and clear. It's the experience of a lifetime."

At Hugh Knox's insistence Alexander went back to his room, got out some paper and a pen, and sat down at his desk to write a story of the hurricane. Working furiously, he finished the composition that evening.

When he returned to the minister's house the next day, Hugh Knox was delighted with his protégé's work. He said that Alexander's style was highly "literary" and "poetic," and that his narrative ability was the finest he had ever seen. He brought his young wife into the study and read the account to her. She declared it a fine, thrilling story.

Hugh Knox's enthusiasm soared even higher. The composition, he said, had to be published. Since no newspaper was printed in English on St. Croix, he took the manuscript and sent it by ship, under Alexander's name, to nearby St. Christopher.

Two weeks passed. One morning Hugh Knox appeared at the counting house and spread open on Alexander's desk the latest edition of the *Royal Danish-American Gazette*. There Alexander saw his "Hurricane Letter" in print.

Styles of writing change greatly from age to age—Alexander's description of the hurricane would not please many of today's newspaper readers. He wrote in a florid and stilted style that was not his own, imitating the worst features of some of the lesser authors he had been reading since he was a boy. He disregarded certain facts and exaggerated others shamelessly.

"Good God!" he wrote. "What horror and destruction—it's impossible for me to describe—or you to form any idea of it. . . . It seemed as if a total dissolution of nature was taking place. The roaring of the sea and wind—fiery meteors flying about in the air—the prodigious glare of almost perpetual lightning—the crash of the falling houses—and the ear-piercing shrieks of the distressed, were sufficient to strike astonishment into Angels. . . ."

Apparently, though, Alexander's "fiery meteors," his "almost perpetual lightning," his "Angels," were not enough to strike astonishment into his readers. The "Hurricane Letter" pleased everyone. Ann Mitchell, quite naturally, declared the first published work of her beloved nephew a masterpiece.

Peter and Mary Lytton agreed that it was a splendid literary achievement, and that any lad of fifteen who could write so well was certainly remarkable.

Their belief in Alexander's talent was strengthened by the favorable comments they began to receive from people outside the family. Close friends, mere acquaintances, even strangers, approached the Mitchells and the Lyttons to congratulate them on their nephew's memorable composition.

Word of the "Hurricane Letter" and of its brilliant young author swept the island. Before long, Governor Walsterstorff himself sent out inquiries to learn more about the boy who had written it.

Locally, at least, Alexander had become famous overnight. And with equal suddenness Peter Lytton now changed his mind about helping to further his nephew's education. He said that he would put up what money he could to send Alexander to college in the American Colonies.

Ann Mitchell had a little money of her own, and she offered to contribute. Friends agreed to add small sums to help defray Alexander's expenses. Though Nicholas Cruger very much wanted to keep Alexander in the business, he was an openhearted man, he had grown fond of his young chief clerk, and he refused in such a matter to consider his own interests. His contribution was large enough so that Alexander's passage to North America and his expenses while at college were provided for.

A family conference was held, at which Hugh Knox was present. He advised Alexander to follow in his own academic footsteps. He himself was a graduate of The College of New Jersey—what is now Princeton University. Alexander agreed to the suggestion and said he would try to enroll there as soon as possible.

Another week and his passage had been booked; in twenty-four hours he was to sail for Boston, on the next ship leaving St. Croix for the American Colonies.

Alexander could hardly believe in his good fortune. Only a few weeks before, he had all but reconciled himself to working for Nicholas Cruger, eventually becoming his partner, and spending the rest of his life as a West Indies merchant. Now, because he had written an article about a hurricane, he was to resume his education, he was to live in a distant country where great political events were said to be in the making, and where, in the bustle and stir of a large city, a young man, alert, capable, ambitious, might rise to startling and unforeseen heights.

By his last afternoon on St. Croix, though, Alexander had grown very sober at the thought of leaving. It was hard enough saying good-bye to his friend and benefactor, Nicholas Cruger. It was even harder saying good-bye to Peter and Mary Lytton on their plantation, and to Ann Mitchell on hers.

On the way back to town he stopped and paid a final visit to the Lyttons' burial ground across the valley. He put flowers on his mother's grave, and for the last time looked down and read her name on the plain stone slab.

He was sure she would have been pleased that he was leaving the Islands to go to college, and this made his coming departure somewhat easier to bear. He thought again of his own good fortune, and of how little good fortune had ever been hers. Then he left the burial ground, unaware that he would never return to that quiet corner of the world again.

The next day he and Hugh Knox took leave of each other beside the waiting ship. Alexander thanked his loyal friend as well as he could, but the list of his debts was too long to recite—he and Hugh Knox shook hands quickly, and then Alexander climbed aboard the ship.

As the lines were cast off and the ship began to edge out of the harbor, Hugh Knox stood on the dock and waved his handkerchief. Minute by minute his figure grew smaller, until finally he could no longer be seen.

The town itself, white and gleaming against the high green hills, soon began to disappear too. Alexander found that his eyes were no longer dry. Though he had done the work of a man for almost four years, he was not yet sixteen, and parting from his home and from those whom he loved was sad and painful.

But before long, youthful pride returned. He wiped at his eyes surreptitiously; he peered around to see if any of the other passengers or the sailors had noticed his tears. They hadn't. The other passengers had gone below. The sailors were too busy coiling rope and setting the sails to pay any attention to him.

Alexander assumed a grave air. No one was going to guess his feelings. No one was going to know that he had been homesick, even before the ship was out of sight of land.

6

---•✦•---

FIRST DAYS IN AMERICA

Aₗₑₓₐₙdₑᵣ and his fellow passengers very nearly failed to
reach Boston. A fire broke out on the voyage and for twenty-
four hours they joined the crew in trying to extinguish it.
Forming a human chain, they passed buckets of sea water
down into the hold and finally the flames were brought under
control. Toward the end of October, 1772, the blackened
ship crept into Boston Harbor, its passengers and crew thank-
ful to be alive.

Alexander did not stay long in Boston. He took a seat on
the first stagecoach to leave for New York, arriving there a
day and a half later after an uncomfortable trip over the
rough, deeply rutted Post Road.

At that time New York City had a population of twenty-
five or thirty thousand people. In area, the city hardly covered
the lower end of Manhattan Island. Its narrow streets were
still unpaved, and when a carriage passed, clouds of yellow
dust filled the air. The city had only a few wells to supply the
inhabitants with fresh water, garbage was thrown into the

streets, and because of the unsanitary living conditions, epidemics broke out frequently.

Nevertheless, to a boy from the West Indies, New York was a marvelous place to see. The city was far larger than Christiansted, and the crowds in the streets moved at a much brisker pace. Perhaps it was the chill autumn air that made everyone walk so quickly—it was certainly the coldest, most invigorating air that Alexander had ever known.

On his arrival he walked along lower Broadway and around the fort and the Governor's house at the southern tip of the island. This was the fashionable part of the city. Along the streets he saw for the first time in his life elegant women in hoopskirts, their hair piled high in ornate curls, and men in richly colored suits and coats of velvet. He saw the neat, old-styled Dutch houses, and the newer and larger brick houses in the English style. He saw fine flower gardens that over-looked the broad Hudson River. He saw more carriages in an hour than he had seen in a year in Christiansted. Throughout the city he found things stirring, an air of excitement, a sense of haste and urgency—and he instantly felt at home in his new surroundings.

That afternoon he looked up Ned Stevens, who helped him find lodgings in the city. Ned took him to dinner several times at Fraunces' Tavern, and introduced him to the faculty and students at Kings College—now Columbia University—where he was studying to become a doctor. Because of Ned, Alexander's first stay in the city was extremely pleasant.

A day or two after his arrival, Alexander visited Kartwright & Company, a firm of merchants. He had with him a letter of credit from Nicholas Cruger. At Kartwright & Company, Alexander was able to draw enough money to meet most of his expenses, and this he continued to do for the next few years, thanks to the generosity of his former employer.

One of the partners in the firm was Hugh Mulligan, who

had a brother, Hercules Mulligan. Alexander was put in the care of Hercules, who took a special liking to the young lad from the West Indies.

Hercules was a tailor, whose clients were mostly rich Tories. When the war came, several years later, Hercules was thought to be a Tory sympathizer. In reality he was an ardent Patriot who often sent information from the city to Washington's Headquarters. After the war Hercules was honored publicly by General Washington, much to the surprise of those who had shunned him during the war.

Through Hercules Mulligan and Ned Stevens, Alexander began to catch a glimpse of what was happening politically in the city and in the rest of the Colonies. Dining with Ned and his young Patriot friends was particularly enlightening, and Alexander hated to leave the city and such lively evenings. But he knew that he had more pressing things to do than to sit at dinner and discuss current affairs; he was in America to resume his education, enter college, and if possible, take up a profession; after a few days of idleness he was anxious to begin.

Shortly afterward he left the city and went to New Jersey. He brought with him a number of letters of introduction which his friend, Hugh Knox, had given him in St. Croix. These letters brought Alexander to the attention of several influential men, particularly Elias Boudinot, a leading Patriot, and William Livingston, a relative of the powerful New York clan of Livingstons, and himself, at that time, the Governor of New Jersey.

Both men were impressed and charmed by Alexander. On their advice he enrolled in a school run by a woman named Frances Barker, in Elizabethtown (now Elizabeth), New Jersey. Here Alexander worked diligently for a year, preparing himself for college.

Now after a man becomes famous there will always be

stories told about him, some of them true, and some of them the distortions and lies circulated deliberately by his enemies. In later years it was sometimes said that Alexander Hamilton had been a snob and a social climber, a poor, untutored, but brilliant young man, who had risen by cold-blooded calculation from the lowest ranks of society to the highest.

The truth was considerably different. Though a lad without money, and a foreigner from the West Indies, he was obviously what was then called "a gentleman." In manners, speech, dress and appearance he belonged to the "gentry," that small and fortunate upper class which was immensely influential in the West Indies and in the Thirteen Colonies at the time of the American Revolution. Elias Boudinot and Governor Livingston invited him into their homes, introduced him to their wives and children, entertained him for days and weeks as their guest, and never thought of him as anything but one of themselves. They enjoyed his wit, good nature and natural charm, his lively and intelligent conversation, and they recognized him as a prodigy. That he came from a lower social class than theirs was an idea that could never have occurred to either the elder Boudinots and Livingstons or to their children.

After a year of tutoring at Elizabethtown, a year in which Alexander also read widely, thanks to the large libraries he found at the Boudinots' and the Livingstons', he decided that he was finally ready to enter college. He journeyed to nearby Princeton and presented himself to President Witherspoon, at Hugh Knox's alma mater, the College of New Jersey.

President Witherspoon approved his application and said that he could enter college at the start of the next term. But Alexander was not satisfied with this. He explained to President Witherspoon that time was important to him, and that he was anxious to advance at his own pace. He asked permission to finish his courses as quickly as possible, without regard for the usual regulations of the college. President Witherspoon said that he could not grant such an unprecedented request without first taking the matter up with his trustees. This he did. Several weeks later the trustees refused flatly to grant permission.

Their refusal proved fortunate for Alexander. He returned to New York City, applied for entrance on the same terms at Kings College, and was accepted there by President Myles Cooper. Instead of remaining for several years in a small, isolated New Jersey town, Alexander moved to the third largest city in the Colonies. In New York there were four daily newspapers that published reports about the political conflicts of the time; there were numerous taverns where Patriot and Loyalist met, debated, and sometimes brawled. New York was a city of change and contrast; it was a melting pot in which merchants, lawyers, sailors, small tradesmen and mechanics all rubbed elbows together, and in which a young man of seventeen, if he had outstanding abilities, might quickly make a mark for himself, as he hardly could hope to do in rural surroundings. Without realizing it at the time, the young scholar owed a debt to the trustees in Princeton for turning him down.

7

COLLEGE DAYS

Alexander hamilton entered Kings College in the fall of 1773. His studies that year included Latin, Greek, mathematics, philosophy, chemistry and anatomy.

At college he found himself among a congenial group of fellow students. Besides Ned Stevens, who left two years later to attend medical school in Edenburgh, his closest friends were Nicholas Fish, Samuel and Henry Nicoll, and Robert Troup. He and Robert Troup became lifelong friends. Many years afterwards, in 1810, Troup published an invaluable account of Hamilton's early years in New York.

Though they worked hard, Hamilton and his college friends did not spend all their time at their studies. One of their favorite extracurricular activities was attending the meetings of a club, which they formed to improve themselves "in composition, debate and public speaking."

Hamilton had never debated before. To his surprise he learned that he not only enjoyed speaking before others, but that he had an exceptional talent for it too. When he rose to his feet, his mind began to fill with ideas, and somehow at the same moment he found the right words to express those ideas, so that they flowed out easily, logically and clearly. Before long it was generally acknowledged that Alexander Hamilton was the best debater and public speaker among the members.

It is not difficult to understand why Hamilton and his classmates formed a club where they could debate the principal issues of the day. Those issues were being argued everywhere in the Thirteen Colonies. The city in which they lived, the colony, the entire countryside from New Hampshire and Vermont in the north to Georgia in the south, seethed with unrest. Hamilton had been a college student only three months, when, on the 16th of December, 1773, the Boston Tea Party took place, inflaming the rebellious spirit of the Colonists. The words "tyranny" and "liberty" were in the air—and the beginning of the war with England was only sixteen months away.

At first it might seem strange that Alexander Hamilton, after only a year on American soil, should have thrown himself wholeheartedly into the cause of the Colonists. But there is really no mystery about it; many of the restrictions placed on the merchants of New York, Philadelphia and Boston by the English Parliament had been placed at the same time on the merchants of Nevis, St. Christopher and St. Croix; many of the oppressive measures which were impoverishing the farmers of the southern colonies were similar to the oppressive measures which had already impoverished many sugar planters in the West Indies. The English system was called "mercantilism"; at its heart was the belief that the products of the West Indies Colonies and the American Colonies should be used in such a way that the merchants of London would benefit handsomely, as indeed they had benefited for more than a century; this "mercantilism" was familiar to

Hamilton from his days at Cruger & Company; his feelings
of resentment against the repressive acts of an English Parliament were identical with the feelings of any patriot in the
American Colonies. In this respect, he was as much at home
in a New York tavern as he would have been in the white
rambling building that overlooked the harbor in Chris-
tiandsted.

After news of the Boston Tea Party reached New York, a
group of Patriots, the New York "Sons of Liberty," decided
to join the rebellious citizens of Massachusetts in their resistance to the new tax on tea. Dock hands refused to unload the
English tea ship anchored in New York Harbor; merchants
refused to purchase the tea, or to allow it to be stored in their
warehouses; finally they compelled the tea ship to leave port
without unloading its cargo.

As the spirit of rebellion spread, as the cry of "No taxation
without representation" was heard more and more often, as
the newspapers printed more and more furious attacks on
the English Parliament and the English Prime Minister, Alexander Hamilton found himself increasingly dissatisfied with
the limited role of a college debater. His brain was teeming
with political ideas and arguments; he remembered that only
a little more than a year before he had written an article for
a newspaper and had met with incredible success. Why not
try again? Why not enter the conflict with his pen, and attack
the Loyalists with whatever eloquence and logic he might
command?

Writing at night and during the day between lectures at
college, he composed his first political article, entitled, "Defense of the Destruction of the Tea," and sent it to *Holt's
Journal* in the city. To his extreme delight it was promptly
published.

Encouraged by this first success, Hamilton wrote a number
of impassioned articles for *Holt's* during the winter and

spring of 1774 which attracted the notice of at least one of New York's leading Patriots. John Jay was thirty years old, and already a figure of prominence on New York's political scene. He had no idea that Alexander Hamilton was only seventeen when he wrote to a friend, Alexander McDougall, "I hope Mr. Hamilton continues busy: I have not received Holt's paper these three months, and therefor cannot judge of the progress he makes." Clearly John Jay had marked Hamilton as a skilled pamphleteer and a useful ally. It was the beginning of what later became a close personal and political association.

By the summer of 1774, the spirit of independence was burning strongly. The British government, following a policy of increasing severity and repression, sought to coerce the Colony of Massachusetts into submission; the government in London had ordered the port of Boston closed to all shipping, and British troops had occupied the city; step by step, the Colonies were being driven into a position which would allow them but two alternatives—surrender to, or open conflict with, the mother country.

Early in July, New York's leaders called a mass meeting to form a plan of joint action to be taken with the other Colonies. On July 6th, a huge crowd slowly gathered in "The Fields," where New York's City Hall Park is now located. A temporary wooden platform had been hurriedly erected for the speakers. John Jay's friend, Alexander McDougall, presided over the open-air meeting. Seated alongside him on the platform were local Patriot leaders. Members of the radical Sons of Liberty were out in full force. Sailors, mechanics, merchants and their apprentices choked The Fields in a solid mass. Loyalists and their sympathizers, all the conservative elements in the city, stayed in their homes, out of harm's way.

Hamilton and his fellow debating club members squeezed through the rough, excited crowd until they were close to the speakers' platform. The speeches began. One after another the Patriot leaders arose and harangued the crowd. Finally Alexander McDougall spoke. He presented a plan, a set of resolutions to prevent the importation of all English goods into the Colonies, until the repressive measures in Boston and elsewhere were rescinded. The resolutions were approved by a huge roar from the crowd.

The meeting was then supposed to end. But it didn't. The crowd wanted more. The club members shouted for another speech as loudly as the mechanics and apprentices surrounding them. Then one of the members shouted, "Give them a speech, Ham! You can do it!" And before he knew it, Hamilton found himself boosted up to the platform by several pairs of hands, while in his ears he heard the cries of "Speech! Speech!" rising on every side.

From his sudden eminence on the platform he could see nothing but the faces of the crowd, hundreds and hundreds of men eagerly awaiting his words. It was a moment that would have challenged the nerve of an experienced public speaker—Hamilton was an amateur. Worse still, he was totally unprepared. He had never dreamed of addressing the rally. For a moment he thought of plunging off the platform and losing himself in the crowd.

Then panic began to leave him. He felt himself filled with a growing excitement, the same kind of excitement that had come over him during the hurricane, as he rode through the wind and the rain to Ann Mitchell's plantation.

He cleared his throat and began. He drew on his articles written for *Holt's Journal;* ideas formed, and the words began to flow swiftly, fiercely, surely. His voice grew stronger, more resonant, as he spoke of the long history of England's repressive acts against her American Colonies: the Sugar Act of 1764, under Prime Minister George Grenville, restricting the free importation of sugar and molasses from the West

Indies; the Currency Act of the same year, prohibiting the printing of paper money in the Colonies; the Quartering Act, which had forced the Colonials to feed and shelter English troops, whether they chose to or not. The hated Stamp Act of 1765, the Laws of Impressment, the laws restricting westward expansion, which denied new farmland to the Colonists. The notorious Townshend Acts, passed by Parliament under the then Prime Minister, "Champagne Charley" Townshend.

To resist such acts of tyranny was the duty of every Colonist, Hamilton insisted. Then he raised his hand and came to the climax—the rising revolt against tyranny would soon become an irresistible tidal wave that would sweep forever from America the ignominious chains and fetters of slavery, leaving the American Colonies gloriously free.

The crowd responded with an immense roar of approval. Everyone clapped, shouted, and demanded to know who the last speaker was. "A collegian!" someone replied. "One of the Kings College boys!"

Hamilton retired from the platform and rejoined his delighted fellow club members. His hand was shaken, his back was pounded with enthusiasm. His maiden speech had been a success.

More important, the afternoon in The Fields brought him forcefully to the attention of all the Patriot leaders on the platform. From that day on, the name of seventeen-year-old Alexander Hamilton was recognized with respect by the leaders of the rebellious party in the city. The young stranger from the West Indies was on his way up in the world.

8

———◦◦———

THE WAR CLOUDS GATHER

In the autumn of 1774, Hamilton and his friends returned
to Kings College for what proved to be their final year of
instruction under Dr. Myles Cooper. During those troubled
months Hamilton did not neglect his studies. Several of his
college exercise books exist today. They contain excerpts—
in Greek, copied from the *Iliad,* as well as many notes taken
from works on ancient geography and history.

At about the time that the fall college term began, the First
Continental Congress was meeting in Philadelphia. In the
Congress there was a struggle for control between the "radicals"—those who were anxious for an open break with
England—and the "conservatives"—those who wanted to move
with great caution and to preserve if possible the existing ties
with England.

The radicals finally won the struggle and forced a resolution
through Congress demanding a complete boycott of all
British goods throughout the Colonies. To enforce the boycott, "committees of inspection" were organized; they were

empowered to use whatever measures were necessary to ensure the boycott's effectiveness—meaning that they had a free hand to fine and punish those who refused to obey the boycott and who purchased British goods.

The Tories were dismayed by these aggressive measures adopted by Congress. They still believed that loyalty and obedience to King and Parliament were not only possible, they were eminently desirable. They believed that if the boycott went into effect, war with England would become inevitable.

During the 1770's, many political pamphlets appeared each month in the Colonies, some written by Tories, some by Patriots. Many of them were published anonymously. The Tories in New York now decided to issue a number of pamphlets, attacking the boycott and other measures approved by Congress.

The best of these Tory pamphlets was one directed at influencing the local farmers. It was an anonymous work, actually written by Dr. Samuel Seabury, a noted Tory churchman. It was called "Free Thoughts on the Proceedings of the Continental Congress," and it was followed almost immediately by another, entitled "Congress Canvassed by a Westchester Farmer," which was also written by Dr. Seabury.

Both pamphlets were skillfully done. They appealed to the farmer's self-interest, pointing out that he had always been generously treated under the English laws, and that he had very little to gain and very much to lose should he support the "rash" acts passed by the Congress in Philadelphia.

The radical Patriots had to reply to these pamphlets with one of their own; while they were still trying to decide who, among their regular pamphleteers, would do the best job, their problem was unexpectedly solved for them. On December 15, 1774, there appeared on the streets of New York a third anonymous pamphlet with the very long title—for such was the style of the day—"A Full Vindication of the Measures of Congress . . . in Answer to a Letter under the Signature of a Westchester Farmer." The pamphlet, though unsigned, had been written by Hamilton. It had been written with the incredible swiftness that more and more came to be his hallmark, and it appeared not long before his eighteenth birthday. In it, almost for the first time, he wrote with much of the simplicity, the force, the clarity and the logic that would distinguish his writings for the remainder of his life.

First, he briefly dealt with the subject of freedom. "The only distinction," he wrote, "between freedom and slavery consists in this: In the former state a man is governed by the laws to which he has given his consent, either in person or by his representative; in the latter, he is governed by the will of another. In the one case, his life and his property are his own; in the other, they depend upon the pleasure of his master. It is easy to discern which of these two states is preferable. No man in his senses can hesitate choosing to be free, rather than a slave."

Then Hamilton went on to discuss the right of Americans to govern themselves. "That Americans are entitled to freedom is incontestable on every rational principal. . . . No reason can be assigned why one man should exercise any power or pre-eminence over his fellow creature more than another; unless they have voluntarily vested him with it. Since . . . Americans have not, by any act of theirs, empowered the British Parliament to make laws for them, it follows they can have no just authority to do it."

Finally Hamilton came to a question in what was later to be his special province—a question of economics. Many Colonists, both Patriot and Tory, feared that the boycott of English goods would harm the Colonies as much as it would harm England. How could the Colonies exist without English goods? they asked. Hamilton said that they could exist without difficulty. Indeed, the Colonists would prosper greatly, he said, if, instead of buying English goods, they learned to manufacture those goods for themselves in America, as they had never been allowed to do under the English laws. "If, by the necessity of the thing," he wrote, "manufacturers should once be established and take root among us, they will pave the way still more to the future glory and grandeur of America."

Already Hamilton was envisioning an industrialized America, an America of machines and factories, a nation that would make its own glass, iron and copperware, and that would export these and a variety of other manufactured products to the rest of the world.

Many years later, the question of America's future development would become a part of the conflict between Hamilton and his great political adversary, Thomas Jefferson. Jefferson would insist that America should remain a nation of small farmers; Hamilton would insist that America should become a nation of industrial workers. The seeds of that future conflict were already planted, and would one day bear fruit.

In a short time, Dr. Seabury returned to the wars with a third pamphlet, attacking Hamilton's "Full Vindication." Still writing anonymously, Hamilton answered Seabury again, by writing and publishing within less than a month, a tract that ran many thousands of words, entitled, "The Farmer Refuted."

Hamilton's two pamphlets were extremely persuasive and did a great deal to make the boycott of English goods effective in New York City and in the surrounding country. Interest ran high as to the identity of their author. At first it was generally supposed that John Jay was the only man who could have written them. But John Jay denied the authorship. When it was finally disclosed that Alexander Hamilton, an eighteen-year-old student at Kings College, had written them, there was a good deal of surprise, and in certain cases, absolute disbelief.

At Kings College, Dr. Cooper, a violent Tory, insisted that Hamilton could not have written the pamphlets without outside help. "He no doubt had the answers from Jay's pen," the President told Hamilton's friend Robert Troup. But, as Troup said later, "I well knew the contrary, as Hamilton wrote the answers when he and I occupied the same room in college, and I read them before they were sent to the press."

There can be little wonder that when John Jay and the other New York Patriots discovered who the author of the two pamphlets really was, they were eager to have him on their side of the conflict, and why they were willing to accept him as a colleague despite his youth.

In a time of public turmoil, with the continual talk of war on every side, Hamilton found it impossible to remain calmly at his desk, studying Greek and Latin, chemistry and anatomy, and in his spare time writing Patriot pamphlets.

Throughout the city the citizens were preparing to take up arms. Muskets were lowered from their wall pegs and cleaned carefully; powder and musket balls were stored and kept ready; squads of Patriots began to drill in the public squares and wherever else they could find room to march.

A former officer in the British Army, Edward Fleming, formed a volunteer company of young New Yorkers, a number of them students from Kings College. Hamilton and his friend Troup were among the first to join. Before classes each morning, they fell in with the others and practiced the manual of arms and learned how to march to a military cadence.

Fleming's company called itself "The Corsicans." The members' uniforms were youthfully gaudy. They wore short green jackets and small round hats, which they sported at a rakish angle. The motto on the crown of their hats was LIBERTY OR DEATH. On their chests they wore a red heart-shaped badge, with the motto, GOD AND OUR RIGHT.

While Hamilton and his fellow Corsicans were busily drilling in the churchyard of St. George's Chapel, the Thirteen Colonies drifted closer and closer to war, and finally into war itself. The battles of Lexington and Concord were fought in Massachusetts; Ethan Allen and his "Green Mountain Boys" from Vermont set out to attack the enemy-held Fort Ticonderoga; in Philadelphia the Second Continental Congress convened to take measures to put the Colonies on a full wartime footing.

Among the delegates from Virginia was Thomas Jefferson, fourteen years older than Hamilton, and already a man highly respected in the other Colonies as well as in his own. At that early time there can be no doubt which of the two future antagonists had the more important position in public affairs—the delegate to Congress who, a year later, would write the first draft of the Declaration of Independence, or the college boy performing the manual of arms in a New York churchyard.

But political prominence for Hamilton lay far in the future. For the present there was study, pamphleteering, and the chance for excitement and adventure.

In the city, after Lexington and Concord, there were frequent riots against the Tories. Dr. Cooper of Kings College soon became a leading target of the rioting mobs. To some extent, at least, he brought his troubles on himself. By openly describing the Sons of Liberty as "a vile rabble," he did little to endear himself to the hearts of the Patriots.

One night Hamilton and Robert Troup were awakened by shouts in the street. Hamilton put his head out of the window and saw a wild-eyed mob passing below. "Where are you going?" he asked.

"To tar and feather Doctor Cooper!" was the reply.

Hamilton told Troup to get dressed quickly. Flinging on their clothes they left their room and took a short cut to the house of Dr. Cooper, who was still sleeping peacefully in his bed. When the mob arrived, Hamilton and Troup were already there, waiting on the porch.

Hamilton shouted for the mob to stop. The mob did. Some of the rioters recognized him as the orator from The Fields, others as the young Patriot pamphleteer and Corsican.

As the rioters hesitated, Hamilton began to harangue them. He told them to give up their project and return quietly to their homes. "Think what you're about to do!" he cried. "The disgrace your conduct will bring to the cause of Liberty! Think—"

At this moment Dr. Cooper, his head in a nightcap, leaned out of the bedroom window. He saw the mob and he saw Hamilton—and he remembered how Troup had once insisted that Hamilton was the author of some violently Patriotic pamphlets.

Hamilton, he thought, is a dangerous Patriot! I know what he's doing here! He's rousing the vile rabble against me!

Dr. Cooper put his head out even further and shouted, "Gentlemen, gentlemen! Don't listen to him! He's crazy! Crazy!" Then he dived back into the bedroom, threw a cloak over his nightshirt, and prepared to rush downstairs to make his escape.

For a moment the mob forgot its anger. Half the rioters doubled over with laughter. This gave Hamilton time to enter the house and find Dr. Cooper. He calmed the old man's fears and managed to slip him safely out by the back door, at the same moment that the mob, urged on by its leaders, was bursting in by the front.

Dr. Cooper was hidden that night at the house of a man named Stuyvesant, and the next night escaped in a small

boat to the *Kingfisher*, an English man-of-war lying in the
harbor. He was not the only Tory to give up his possessions
and property and leave the Colonies during the war. In all,
over fifty thousand Colonists left the country, many fleeing
north to the safety of Canada.

It was significant that Hamilton, though an ardent Patriot,
should nevertheless have risked the fury of a mob to save the
most notorious Tory in the city from violence. He had done
so, in part, because he liked and respected his teacher and
wanted to keep the elderly man safe from harm. But there
was another reason. Although Hamilton detested Dr. Cooper's
political opinions, he detested far more the unlawful acts of
a mob of rioters. Lawlessness in any form aroused his disgust;
with the passing years it became more and more a basic tenet
of his political faith that human happiness is only possible
in a country where the law is reverenced and obeyed.

With the departure of Dr. Cooper, Kings College shut its
doors for the duration of the American Revolution. Hamilton kept up his wide reading, though; he continued to study
books on history, finance, and political economy, and to
these subjects he added another: the science of gunnery.

Soon some of the Corsicans found themselves in action.
The city was not yet occupied, but several British warships,
including the *Asia,* were at anchor in the bay. A rumor
swept the city that sailors and marines would land from the
ships to seize the twenty-one giant cannons that were em-
placed in the fort, called The Battery, at the southern tip of
Manhattan Island.

On the night of the 23rd of August, 1775, a militia company, under Captain John Lamb, joined by a band of
civilians, approached The Battery. Their object was to re-
move the cannons to keep them from falling into enemy
hands. Several Corsicans, among them Hamilton, Robert

Troup and Hamilton's old friend Hercules Mulligan, joined in the work.

An armed barge was sent out from the *Asia*. It discovered the crowd at the fort and began to fire on it. Some of Captain Lamb's men returned the fire with their muskets. Soon there was a brisk battle underway.

The drums of the city rolled furiously, sounding the general alarm. A battalion of regular troops under Colonel Lasher arrived and opened fire on the barge. The guns of the *Asia* began to bombard The Battery.

Hamilton and Troup and Hercules Mulligan pulled at one of the great cannons. They finally hauled it away from the fort to safety, through a hail of fire; the other twenty cannons were rescued too.

Only after reaching safety, away from the harbor, did Hamilton realize that he had left his musket behind in the excitement. The Battery was still under bombardment from the *Asia*. Hamilton raced back to The Battery, found his musket, and retreated to safety a second time.

Three men on shore were wounded that night and one man was killed on the *Asia*'s barge. The smoky fields of battle, which the young clerk in Nicholas Cruger's counting house had dreamed about, were now a reality. Alexander Hamilton had found his war.

9

CAPTAIN HAMILTON AND
MAJOR BURR

O N the 6th of January, 1776, the New York Provincial Congress decided that an artillery company should be formed to aid in the defense of the Colony. This was the chance that Hamilton had been waiting for. As soon as he heard the news he applied for a commission and for command of the company.

The New York Congress was not eager to hand a captain's commission to an inexperienced youth of nineteen. Some of Hamilton's friends had to bring their influence to bear before it was agreed that Hamilton would go before a board of examiners to prove his qualifications. At the inquiry, he answered the board's questions and convinced the members that he was both fit for the responsibility and able to perform the required duties. The board said that very shortly the captaincy would be his.

In early March, while he was still awaiting his commission,

Hamilton's friend Elias Boudinot arrived in great excitement from New Jersey. William Alexander, another of Boudinot's friends, had just been appointed the commanding general of the Continental or "regular" forces in New York. Boudinot had spoken to him and had secured a position for Hamilton on the general's staff, with the rank of brigade major.

Politely but firmly, Hamilton refused the appointment. He explained to the well-meaning Boudinot that he was expecting his commission as militia captain at any time. Though brigade major was a higher rank than captain, and the opportunity of serving on the general's staff a fine one, he preferred the lower rank because it carried with it the chance to serve in combat as an officer of the line. With great battles bound to come soon, and with military glory so close at hand, he had no intention of sitting things out in the rear. Poor Boudinot had to swallow his disappointment and return to New Jersey with a tactful explanation for the general, whose generous offer had been refused.

A week later, on March 14th, orders arrived from the New York Congress appointing Alexander Hamilton a "Captain of the Provincial Company of the Artillery of this Colony."

Captain Hamilton was immediately beset by difficulties. To begin with, he received his guns from the public stores, but he was given no soldiers. At that time the commander of a militia company was expected to enlist his men at his own expense, paying the soldiers a bounty for enlisting, and purchasing all of their clothing and equipment. Hamilton used every penny he could lay his hands on, and within a few days he had a fully uniformed company of thirty men, with several dozen more ready to sign up too.

The next problem he faced was that of turning his untrained civilians into soldiers. During the Revolutionary War, the militiamen of the various Colonies made notoriously poor troops. They resented discipline, they sometimes refused to fight or to obey orders, and if the weather was too bad or living conditions too severe—and often living conditions were severe indeed—they deserted in droves.

At first Hamilton's company was no better than the rest of the New York militia. A couple of his sergeants and corporals had to be tried for mutiny, and were reduced to privates. Some of his men were also tried for disobedience to orders and for desertion. Nevertheless, Hamilton remained firm; the boy who had drilled his schoolmates so relentlessly on St. Croix was now a man who drilled his soldiers relentlessly in New York. But he was a just officer and his men quickly came to respect him. He gave them the best clothing obtainable, he fought to get them a promotion when he thought they deserved one, and he forced the New York Congress to pay them what they were entitled to.

Slowly word spread that Captain Hamilton's artillery company was worth watching. High-ranking officers in command of Continental troops passed by The Fields and stopped to observe the militia in training. One company stood out for the fine appearance of its equipment and for the soldierly bearing of its men. Captain Hamilton was put down as a young officer who got things done. A number of colonels and generals decided to keep an eye on him in the future.

In June, Hamilton was ordered to Bowling Green, at the south end of Manhattan Island, where he placed his guns so that they would command the harbor. The British were expected to attack the city, and they were not long in coming. On the 12th of July, the British Army arrived by ship, escorted by their fleet, led by the *Phoenix* and the *Rose*.

When the fleet sailed up The Narrows and anchored in New York Harbor, Hamilton ordered his guns into action. Their luck was poor that day. None of the British warships was damaged, but one of Hamilton's guns burst as it was being fired and two of his cannoneers were killed.

General William Howe, the English commander-in-chief, successfully landed his well-disciplined army of thirty-four thousand men on Staten Island, to the south of Manhattan, on the far side of the harbor. His orders were to crush the rebellion, and he seemed to be in an excellent position to do so.

George Washington, the American commander-in-chief, had just arrived from Boston with a small, undisciplined, ill-equipped army to oppose Howe. General Washington's position was desperate from the beginning. Militarily, it was folly to defend Manhattan Island, especially with the British Fleet in complete control of the surrounding waters, but for political reasons, Washington was obliged to attempt a defense; he knew that some of the Colonies were wavering in their willingness to fight the British; the loss of New York City, particularly without a fight, might well persuade those Colonies to abandon the struggle.

The first thing that Washington did was to demand that various New York militia companies be made a part of the Continental Army, so that they would be under his orders. The Continental Congress in Philadelphia and the New York Congress both passed resolutions in favor of Washington's demand. As a result, on the 9th of August, Hamilton's company and the rest of the New York militia became regular troops. Hamilton's company was assigned to General Scott's brigade.

By the last part of August, General Howe's plan was more or less clear. He would land his army somewhere in Brooklyn, push north to Brooklyn Heights, and from the high ground there, rain cannon shot on Washington's helpless troops stationed on lower ground in Manhattan. The latter would have to retreat northward to Harlem and perhaps as far as Westchester, or surrender where they were; in either case, the city would fall into British hands.

To prevent this, Washington divided his already limited forces: one part he kept in Manhattan under his direct command; the other part he sent across the East River to defend Brooklyn Heights.

Hamilton ferried his guns across to the Heights and saw at once that the position was nearly hopeless. He wrote a hurried letter to Washington: to attempt to defend the Heights, with the British Fleet in a position to fire on them from the harbor, and with General Howe's vastly greater army in a position to attack them from farther down the shore, was to invite complete disaster; far better to retreat back across the East River before the British could attack, abandon southern Manhattan and the city, and take up a line of defense to the north.

Hamilton gave the letter to his friend Hercules Mulligan, who gave it to the regimental commander, Colonel Webb. It is not known if Colonel Webb forwarded the letter, or, if he did, whether Washington even had time to read it.

Almost at once, on the 27th of August, Howe attacked. He landed his army in Brooklyn, but farther from Manhattan than Washington had anticipated, where there were no defending American troops. Howe's soldiers poured inland, swiftly broke the American left flank at Jamaica, and drove it back in panic on the main body at Brooklyn Heights.

Had Howe moved decisively that day, he could easily have destroyed the American forces in Brooklyn, while Washington, in Manhattan, could have done nothing to prevent the slaughter. Such an American catastrophe would probably have ended the Revolutionary War before it had really begun.

But William Howe was a general who sometimes delayed the movement of his army for no apparent reason. Now he decided to withhold his attack until the following morning, and this gave the Americans, despite their desperate position, a slim chance to escape.

Late in the afternoon, Washington issued orders: his soldiers in Brooklyn were to retreat to Manhattan, under the cover of darkness.

Luck was with the Americans that night. At dusk, a thick mist settled over the East River. A heavy rain began to fall. The night was pitch-black, and the British sailors failed to see any movement on the water. The wind rose, drowning out the whispers of the men and the splash of their oars. The American soldiers were soaked by the waves that poured into their barges and small boats, but their movements remained undetected. By dawn they had made the crossing safely, without a shot being fired at them by the British Fleet.

When Hamilton and his company had gotten their guns back to Manhattan, they dragged them into position at a small fort called Bunker's Hill, not far from the southern end of the island. Other troops gathered at the fort, although by now Washington and the main body of Americans were already several miles to the north, at Harlem Heights.

Howe soon landed on Manhattan, at Kip's Bay; his landing threatened to cut off all the soldiers remaining in the south from Washington's main army in Harlem.

At Bunker's Hill, everything was in confusion. The senior officer present, General Henry Knox, was unable to make up his mind what to do. One moment he said that their only hope was to abandon the fort and retreat at once. The next moment he said that retreat was already impossible. They were all to remain at the fort, and sell their lives as dearly as possible.

Then a young major named Aaron Burr burst into the fort. He was a year older than Hamilton, had the same slim build, and was an inch shorter than Hamilton's five-foot-seven. He was equally ambitious, equally precocious, and in certain ways, equally gifted.

As far as anyone knows, this was the first time that Hamilton and Burr had ever met. In later years they would meet often, their mutual antagonism would grow, they would become the bitterest of enemies. On this day, though, in the confusion of the fort, Burr could scarcely have noticed his future rival.

Burr went to the commanding officer, General Knox, and demanded to know what he was waiting for. Didn't the general realize there wasn't a moment to lose if he wanted to lead his men to safety?

General Knox was very fat and very tired. The idea of remounting his horse and attempting to reach safety by riding through the entire British Army did not appeal to him. The general said he was going to make a stand in the fort, and hold the place at all costs.

Aaron Burr turned to the soldiers. It was an act of insubordination, but under the circumstances it may have been justified. He said the fort couldn't hold out twenty minutes. He said he knew the back roads, and could lead them all to safety if they were willing to follow him at once. Otherwise, they would have no choice but to remain at the fort and be killed or taken prisoner. The soldiers raised a shout, ignored General Knox and some of their own officers, and said they would follow Major Burr wherever he would lead them.

Burr put himself in command, and the other officers, including General Knox, followed him meekly from the fort.

Burr knew the back roads as well as he had claimed. He took the party north, avoided the British except for a single cavalry patrol which was beaten off, and finally led the way into the main lines at Harlem Heights without losing a man.

During the flight, Hamilton's men had to abandon their baggage, most of their personal possessions, their cannon shot, and one of their guns. Hamilton must have been impressed by Burr's coolness and daring. His respect for Burr, though, was probably tinged with youthful jealousy. He himself had dreamed for years of the glories of war and of the chance to act with courage and daring in the face of disaster and death. But when the chance had come, he not only had let it slip through his fingers, he had seen another man, his own age, seize it fearlessly and turn it to his own credit. Perhaps Aaron Burr did not remember Alexander Hamilton after their flight to Harlem; it seems certain that Hamilton remembered Burr all too well.

10

AT THE FRONT

Bᴜᴛ Hamilton soon had an opportunity to prove his own courage and daring. General Howe, moving at a leisurely pace, finally attacked at Harlem Heights and forced Washington's army to retreat northward again. The Americans withdrew to White Plains, in Westchester, and here, for the first time, Hamilton's company came under heavy fire.

Washington's army occupied two hills at White Plains. The higher one, on the left, was Chatterton's Hill, the key to the entire position. It was here that the chief attack was almost sure to come.

Along the base of the two hills ran the Bronx River. Usually it was only a gently flowing stream, no more than three or four feet deep. But now it was swollen by heavy rains so that it could not be easily forded.

Howe's troops were British regulars and notorious Hessians, German mercenaries that England used during much of the war against her rebellious colonies.

Hamilton was ordered to take up a position on the flank

of Chatterton's Hill, from where his guns could cover the banks of the swollen stream. Before long the Hessians, commanded by Colonel Rahle, began to attack. They advanced through an open field to the stream, while engineers began to throw a wooden bridge across it. Hamilton's two guns could not fire on the bridge because of an intervening rise of ground; he ordered the guns hauled up to a higher position. The guns were hardly placed there and their muzzles lowered, when the bridge was thrown across the stream and the first Hessians started to race over with fixed bayonets, to charge up the hill.

Hamilton ordered his guns to fire, to reload, to fire again. Several engineers, trying to strengthen the bridge supports, were killed in the stream. Several Hessians dropped in their ranks. The guns fired again and again. The Hessians wavered in the charge, broke ranks and fled down the hill and across the bridge to the opposite bank.

Meanwhile some British regulars had crossed the stream at a point below the bridge. They came storming up the hill from the other side, hoping to reach Hamilton's position and spike his guns.

Hamilton ordered the guns swung around. He opened fire on the charging British soldiers, while from a higher position on the hill the entrenched American infantry opened a heavy crossfire with their muskets. Cannon and musket proved too much for the British. They retreated down the side of Chatterton's Hill in the direction of the wooden bridge.

But there was no rest for Hamilton's men. Colonel Rahle had already rallied his Hessians, and they came forward again, recrossed the bridge, and linked up with the retiring British. The British reformed their ranks, and then the two bodies of troops broke into separate columns and charged up the hill at the guns, from two directions.

This second assault unnerved the Americans. The infantry

broke and fled, leaving Hamilton and his company alone to face the enemy. Hamilton was ordered to retire from his exposed position. Luckily some American reinforcements came up just then and began to cover his retreat. He was able to get his guns away only seconds before the Hessians and the British stormed into the abandoned position.

For the rest of that autumn Washington had no choice but to retreat with his army before the superior British forces. From White Plains he withdrew to North Castle; from North Castle he ferried his army across the Hudson River to New Jersey; in New Jersey he turned south, still in retreat.

His army was even smaller now than it had been in the early summer when he had reached Manhattan. His discouraged soldiers, defeated in every battle they had fought, with much of their supplies and equipment lost to the enemy, were deserting in great numbers. Four or five thousand officers and men, all that Washington had left under his command, retreated southward through New Jersey to the banks of the Raritan River. Close behind them, at the head of eight thousand fresh, well-equipped troops, came a new British general, Lord Cornwallis.

Washington and his army got safely across the river and burned the main bridge behind them. To force the British to delay their crossing, Washington left a small rear guard at the river. Hamilton's company was assigned to it.

Hamilton placed his two guns in concealment near the river, and waited. The British soldiers came down to the river, which was low enough to be forded. When they had reached the middle of the river, where the current was strongest, Hamilton opened fire. The British withdrew in confusion to the far bank. They reformed their ranks, brought up some of their own artillery and, under the cover of the shelling, plunged into the water again. As they finally forced a passage to the near side, Hamilton hauled his guns away from the riverbank, and fled to safety. By then, Washington's weary army had gained a breathing space. His scouts were already entering Princeton, fifteen or twenty miles to the south.

Most of the American troops straggled into Princeton without any semblance of order or military precision. But not Hamilton's company. The months of relentless drilling showed itself in the brisk and efficient way his men handled the guns and in the soldierly appearance they made as they marched in step down Nassau Street. Washington asked for the name of the young officer in charge of the company, and then told an aide to invite Captain Hamilton to Headquarters the next time there was a prolonged halt in the march. What happened at their first meeting is not known, but from later events it seems clear that Hamilton made a favorable impression on the General.

By November, 1776, Washington's badly mauled army made camp in Pennsylvania, across the Delaware River from New Jersey. The Hessians went into winter quarters at Trenton, on the other side of the river. On Christmas night, Hamilton's company took part in one of the most famous exploits of the Revolutionary War. While the Hessians were enjoying a huge banquet, Washington ferried his troops across the ice-clogged Delaware River, about eight miles above Trenton. He split his forces into two columns, one under General John Sullivan, the other under General Nathanael Greene. They descended on Trenton and caught the Hessians completely by surprise. Colonel Rahle was killed and nine hundred Hessians taken prisoner. The victory, after so many months of defeat, did a great deal to revive the spirits of the weary Americans. It also encouraged enlistments the following spring.

Pushing north, Washington attacked a part of Cornwallis' troops at Princeton, on January 3, 1777. Some British soldiers had taken cover in Nassau Hall, the main building of the College of New Jersey. Hamilton brought his guns to bear on the building and ordered the soldiers to surrender. They refused. The first shot from Hamilton's guns went through the chapel and scored a direct hit on a painting of the late English king, George II. The next shot fell among the British soldiers, who surrendered soon afterwards. If Hamilton did not attend classes in Princeton, he at least left the college there something to remember him by.

After the victories at Trenton and Princeton, Washington withdrew his meager forces into winter quarters at Morristown, New Jersey. The commander-in-chief had long been troubled with an administrative problem, and now, during the lull in the fighting, he moved to solve it.

His problem was that he needed a capable and trustworthy secretary, an officer who could handle the immense and ever-increasing paper work at Headquarters. He needed a fluent writer to take charge of his correspondence with various Colonial Legislatures, with the separate sections of the Continental Armies, and with the Continental Congress in Philadelphia.

Washington had a number of young aides on his staff, all active and courageous officers, but they were more talented with a musket or a saber than they were with a pen. Washington had already tried out most of them as secretary, with poor results. Where could he find a capable young officer who would be able to ease the burden of paper work from his shoulders?

General Nathanael Greene had seen a certain Captain Hamilton near the banks of the Raritan River, ably working his guns against the attacking British. He had recommended Hamilton to General Washington for his gallantry in the river action. Washington had already noticed Hamilton in

Princeton, and had talked with him briefly. Now Washington made further inquiries. He learned that Hamilton had been a college student in New York, that he had written some notable political pamphlets, that he was an able writer, wrote logically and with great speed, and that he had an exceptionally clear and invaluable understanding of the political situation in the Colonies. Washington summoned Hamilton to his quarters and "asked" the twenty-year-old captain if he would be willing to join his staff as one of his aides-de-camp? He would serve as the General's private secretary, with the rank of lieutenant colonel.

Almost anyone else would have stammered out his acceptance immediately. The offer was a fine one—to rise from captain to lieutenant colonel overnight; to leave the dangers, the sweat, the obscurity of the front lines and to exchange them for the glamour and prestige of the General's staff. How could an offer be made more alluring?

But it wasn't alluring to Hamilton. He had already refused the staff appointment which his friend Elias Boudinot had secured for him, in order that he might see action. After a year in the field, Hamilton wanted to remain in the front ranks until he had proved to his own satisfaction that there was no more capable or courageous officer than himself. His obsession with military glory was still not appeased, and so he desperately wanted to refuse Washington's offer.

He said he was flattered, which was true. He begged for time to consider his reply. He delayed, and then delayed further. But there was no escape. An "invitation" from General Washington might be offered with the warmest smiles and the most polite phrases—it was still a command.

Unwillingly, with a reluctance that was both whimsical and childish, Hamilton finally announced that he would accept the post. On March 1, 1777, Alexander Hamilton was commissioned a lieutenant colonel in the Continental Army, and joined Washington's staff as the General's aide-de-camp and private secretary. It was the beginning of an association that would last more than twenty years, and that would have a profound effect on the country's future.

11

THE BEGINNING
OF A STATESMAN

GENERAL WASHINGTON was soon convinced that he had made a wise choice in selecting Hamilton to be his secretary. He had only to make his wishes known, to state his ideas about a given subject, and the matter was promptly taken care of. Military orders, requisitions, letters to other generals or to members of Congress—Hamilton drafted them quickly, showed them to Washington and, with his approval, made fresh copies and sent them off. A happy arrangement for the General, but one that rarely pleased his aide during the next four years.

Hamilton never lost his taste for military action. He missed his artillerymen and his cannons, and the life of a front-line soldier. Nor did he like to do routine work, whether it was for Nicholas Cruger in a West Indies counting house or for General Washington at Army Headquarters. He always felt that putting another man's ideas on paper was a poor way to

spend one's time, and being a lieutenant colonel and confer-
ring each day with the commander-in-chief did not satisfy his
restless nature.

Ever since he had been a boy of twelve, with his own fortune to make in the world, Hamilton had been ambitious.
But it was only during his military service that his ambition
slowly began to take a new direction.

There, before his very eyes, was the fascinating spectacle of
a nation struggling to be born. Would that birth be successful? Would the few bedraggled Colonial soldiers prove strong
enough to defeat the superior British Army and win independence for the Thirteen Colonies?

And if they were successful in battle, if a new nation
emerged, what sort of nation would it be? What kind of government should it have? How would it manage its internal
affairs, its foreign relations? What men would guide the new
nation, and what means should they use to ensure its future
prosperity and strength?

These were the questions that Hamilton considered during
his service in the Revolutionary Army. And as he thought
about them, he began to wonder what part he himself might
be able to play in the development of the new nation.

As a pamphleteer, he had already learned that he could
sway public opinion. He had a few highly placed friends—
John Jay in New York, Elias Boudinot and William Livingston in New Jersey—who could help him advance in political
life if he chose to enter it. And as a member of Washington's
personal staff he was beginning to meet and to correspond
with other important men who might be useful to him in
the future.

He came to see that for years past, without having realized
it at the time, he had been reading and studying in just those
fields—history, economics, and social and political philosophy
—where an extensive knowledge and understanding would

qualify a man for positions of public trust and responsibility. Reading, indeed, was one of the most important things that Hamilton ever did, both as a boy and as a young man, to prepare himself for the greatness which he had always dreamed about.

Constant study was his lifelong habit. No matter what physical handicaps he had to overcome, he never stopped reading. Years before, at Frederiksted, he had forced himself to read at night after a full day's work, despite the cockroaches, the mosquitoes, and the centipedes. In the army, despite forced marches, the heat and cold, the whistling flight of Hessian musket balls, he forced himself, at the end of the day, to read a few pages by the light of a guttering candle.

There still exists a copy of Hamilton's army paybook. On the margin of some of its pages the young soldier jotted down the names of the books that he read during the campaigns. The books included the works of Demosthenes, Cicero and Plutarch; Bacon's *Essays*, Hobbes' *Dialogues*, and, a characteristic touch, a volume called *Dictionary of Trade and Commerce*.

Hugh Knox had once thought that poetry was the field in which Hamilton was destined to distinguish himself. Hugh Knox was wrong, of course. The art of government was the field in which Hamilton's talents really lay. And already at White Plains, at the Raritan, at Trenton and at Morristown, many of Hamilton's basic political ideas were taking shape.

In the same paybook there is the following passage, copied in his neat hand, from the *First Philippic* of Demosthenes: "As a general parades at the head of his troops, so . . . ought politicians . . . to march at the head of affairs; insomuch that they ought not to wait the event, to know what measure to take; but the measures which they have taken, ought to proclaim the event."

By now, Hamilton was thinking of America's future government—and he had decided there should be a strong executive at the head of it, a man who could "march at the head of affairs . . . as a general at the head of his troops." Here was one of Hamilton's chief political ideas, and it was already formed in the mind of the young soldier.

Hamilton had not served long as Washington's secretary before he received an invitation that was to have far-reaching consequences for him. The invitation was issued by three of New York's leading citizens, Robert R. Livingston, Gouverneur Morris and William Allison. It was issued on behalf of the New York Convention, the political body then ruling the Colony. The three men wrote a joint letter to Hamilton, explaining that the Convention was anxious to keep in touch with conditions at Washington's Headquarters and have put in its hands any information that concerned the progress of the war. Would Hamilton, as a citizen of New York, be willing to become the correspondent of the Convention and, by writing a daily letter, keep the members informed?

Hamilton knew the real reason for the invitation. New York, like all of the Colonies, was jealous of any authority except its own. The Colonies did not trust Congress in Philadelphia, and kept it weak, because they could not always control its actions. The Colonies did not trust General Washington, because his military power was independent of theirs. The Colonies could not prevent the commander-in-chief from running the war, but they wanted to know what he was doing at every step, and they wanted to be sure that his power did not increase at the expense of their own.

Hamilton also knew that two of his friends and fellow aides at Headquarters, Tench Tilghman and Robert Harrison, had previously acted as correspondents to the New York Convention, but that they had quickly tired of the task. Hamilton said he would gladly undertake it. Soon he was sending off a daily letter to New York.

Hamilton's letters were supposed to deal only with military questions. But the members of the Convention were deeply impressed by the force and logic of what Hamilton wrote, and so they began to ask for his opinions on political matters as well. After several weeks, Gouverneur Morris sent Hamilton a draft of the proposed New York Constitution and asked the twenty-year-old officer for his comments. Robert Livingston seconded the request. In a letter to Livingston, sent from Morristown on May 19, 1777, Hamilton gave his opinions on the New York State Constitution.

"I partly agree and partly disagree with you respecting the deficiencies of your Constitution," Hamilton told Livingston. Then he went on to elaborate, writing such things as, "That there is a want of vigor in the executive I believe will be found true. . . . A representative democracy . . . will in my opinion be most likely to be happy, regular and durable. . . . The evil I mean is, that in time your Senate . . . will be liable to degenerate into a body purely aristocratical. . . . I think your Government far the best that we have yet seen, and capable of giving long and substantial happiness to the people."

Through such letters as this, Hamilton called his talents and his political views to the attention of four of New York's richest and most powerful men—Robert Livingston, Gouverneur Morris, William Duer and Philip Schuyler. One by one they began to correspond with Hamilton, as private citizens as well as in their capacity of public officials. They came to depend on his strength of mind and force of character and they began to draw on his ideas, which so often paralleled their own. A personal bond was established and Hamilton, despite his youth, was recognized as an intellectual and political equal by all four men. General Philip Schuyler in particular became a fervent admirer of Hamilton, with a result, three years later, which neither man could have foreseen.

The entire New York Convention came to rely on Hamilton's judgment, and sometimes his influence with the Convention members proved useful to Washington. Several of the Colonies, including New York, grew impatient with Washington's conduct of the war. Why did Washington retreat so often, why did he refuse, again and again, to take a stand in the open and fight it out with the British?

Hamilton wrote a crisp note to Robert Livingston explaining the reasons. The liberty of America was an infinite prize, he said, too precious to risk foolishly. "We should not play a desperate game for it," he wrote, "or put it upon the issue of a single cast of the die. The loss of one general engagement may effectually ruin us." Livingston and the other members swallowed their impatience and stopped their complaints. Thanks to Hamilton, in large measure, New York did not join some of her sister colonies in howling for the General's scalp.

12

THE "LITTLE LION"

Hamilton's letters to the New York Convention, of course, had nothing to do with his official military duties. They were written, along with personal letters to Hugh Knox, Ann Mitchell and Nicholas Cruger, in his "spare time." For Hamilton wrote quickly and tirelessly, and he rarely allowed his pen or his mind to remain inactive.

There was also a lighter side to life at Washington's Headquarters. Local belles sometimes came to the camp and expected to be danced with, entertained at dinner and escorted around the encampment by the light of the stars. When the ladies were absent, Hamilton and his fellow aides traded jokes with one another and discussed military questions at the General's table.

Hamilton was soon a favorite among Washington's younger officers. A number of them became his close friends. There was Robert Harrison, who first decided that Hamilton, because of his small size and his thirst for military action, should be called the "Little Lion"—a nickname that stuck in camp.

There was Tench Tilghman, who had quickly grown tired of reporting to the New York Convention. There was Richard Meade, and later, when they had joined Washington's staff, James McHenry and John Laurens. They, like Hamilton's schoolmates in Christiansted, admired their companion's intense energy, his intelligence and wit, and his bubbling good humor. And Hamilton was always grateful for pleasant companions. He worked hard and spent long hours at his desk; but when work was over, he enjoyed a good dinner with wine and clever talk, a table filled with pretty women and worldly men, a glass or two of whiskey afterwards to conclude the evening. Thanks to the young ladies who visited the camp, and to his friends among the officers, Hamilton was able to bear more easily the discouragement that everyone felt as the months dragged by and the course of the war showed no improvement.

The spring and summer of 1777 was a discouraging time for the cause of American freedom. In Europe, England's chief rival, France, continued to watch events from the sidelines, preferring to be sure that the Colonies had a reasonable chance of success before going to their assistance.

In America, the British were on the attack in two sectors. General John Burgoyne was leading an army south from Canada, with the aim of reaching Albany and cutting off New England from the rest of the Colonies. General Howe, using his powerful fleet to transport part of his army, had sailed from New York toward the coast of Maryland. Howe hoped that by landing in Maryland and attacking Philadelphia, where Congress was then in session, he could force Washington to lead his smaller army out of the New Jersey hills, to protect Congress and the city. In the hills, Washington and his army were impregnable. Out in the open, on the plains, Howe was sure he could defeat the Americans in a pitched battle.

At first Washington refused to budge. He kept his troops deployed in the uplands, and declined to rush to Philadelphia's defense. Hamilton, writing to Hugh Knox, explained Washington's strategy in this way.

"It may be asked," he wrote, "if, to avoid a general engagement, we give up objects of the first importance [like Philadelphia], what is to hinder the enemy from carrying every important point, and ruining us? My answer is, that our hopes are not placed in any particular city or spot of ground, but in preserving a good army, furnished with proper necessaries, to take advantage of favorable opportunities and defeat the enemy by piecemeal."

But Washington was forced to abandon his strategy, against his own better judgment. The people of Philadelphia demanded that he defend their city. More important, the members of Congress demanded it too. Washington had to move his army south to meet the British, as they drove north from where they had landed in Maryland on the 25th of August. Twenty-five miles southwest of Philadelphia the opposing armies collided at Brandywine. After a fierce battle, Washington's smaller forces had to give up the field and retreat once more.

As the British moved on to seize Philadelphia, and as Washington's army retired toward the hills which it never should have left, Hamilton found himself taking part in an adventure that pleased him greatly and that kept his nickname of the "Little Lion" alive in camp.

Washington's soldiers were retreating so quickly that they didn't have time to carry away with them certain army supplies stored along the main road to Philadelphia. To keep these supplies out of the enemy's hands, Washington sent Hamilton and another officer, Captain Henry Lee, at the head of a band of eight cavalrymen, to destroy the mills where the supplies were lying. The mission promised to be dangerous because the British were using the same road and might reach the mills at any moment.

Hamilton welcomed the danger and the chance to perform in the field again. Free from his duties as secretary, he could hardly wait to get started. While it was still early morning he set off with his small troop of horsemen. Before them, the ground rose slowly; after a ride of several miles they drew up their panting horses. Below them they saw the mills, filled with the army supplies that had to be destroyed. A swift stream raced by the mills, a narrow wooden bridge spanning it. Not far off, the stream flowed into the broad Schuylkill River, which gleamed with flashes of sunlight.

No British troops were in sight. Hamilton, though a fearless soldier, was also a prudent one. He sent two of his men to high ground near the mills, to act as lookouts. Then, giving the signal, he galloped down to the mills.

Again Hamilton acted with caution. He divided his men into two groups and sent one group, under Captain Lee, to secure a small, flat-bottomed boat he had seen lying near the bank of the Schuylkill. Then, on the run, he led the other group to the mills, lit torches, and began to set fire to the supplies.

Hamilton was inside one of the mills, putting the torch to some barrels of flour, when he heard muskets being fired. He ran out of the mill, ordering his men to follow. Looking around, he saw the two lookouts riding full speed down the hill, and right at their heels, a large number of British cavalrymen.

The lookouts thundered over the wooden bridge and spurred on to the Schuylkill. Captain Lee and his two soldiers had returned to the mills with their horses. They remounted and raced after the lookouts to the riverbank. All five riders spurred their horses into the water, and the animals carried them to the safety of the opposite shore.

Hamilton and his four men had no time to untie their horses, mount them, and flee. Instead they ran to the river-bank, jumped into the flat-bottomed boat, cut the rope that secured it, and pushed off into the river, escaping only seconds before the first British soldiers reached the spot.

The Schuylkill was running high and the little boat, badly overloaded, was tossed around like a chip of wood, now this way, now that, in the swift currents. Captain Lee, safe on the other side, rose in his saddle. He saw the boat turn and dip, the British firing into it from the shore; then a single shot returned from the boat. Again the British fired into the boat, but this time there was no answering fire from Hamilton or his men. Then the road turned away from the river and Lee saw and heard no more.

Lee rode back toward his own lines, and as soon as he was sure he was beyond pursuit, sent a message to Washington describing their misfortune and saying that it seemed certain that Colonel Hamilton and his men had either been shot or had been drowned in the river.

Washington, who not only had come to respect Hamilton for his intelligence but had also come to like and admire the restless energy of his young aide, had just received the message and was reading it when the flap of his tent parted. In came Hamilton, dripping from head to foot, his uniform torn and muddy, to blurt out the news that Captain Lee was probably drowned or captured. He himself had been lucky to steer his little boat to safety, although one of his men had been killed by the British fire and another man had been severely wounded.

That night, at the General's table, Hamilton and Lee were together, and everyone talked of their exploit in escaping from the British. The Little Lion had shown his mettle, and his fellow aides—Tench Tilghman, John Laurens, all of them—talked of nothing but Hamilton's bravery, mixing sly jokes in with their praise. Such a night was sweet to Hamilton. No doubt it was one of the most satisfying moments he knew during the war.

13

---◆◆◆---

THE "HERO OF SARATOGA"

AFTER the American defeat at Brandywine, the British under General Howe marched on Philadelphia. Hamilton wrote a hasty letter to John Hancock, the President of the Continental Congress, advising him that the city faced imminent capture. There was a great panic in the city following the arrival of Hamilton's letter. Some members of Congress, like John Adams of Massachusetts, were awakened in their beds at three in the morning and told that British troops were at the gates of the city. The members, forgetting their dignity, packed their belongings and fled while it was still dark outside. They rode west, as far as Lancaster, Pennsylvania, where the next congressional sessions were held.

But there was no need for such haste. General Howe, as usual, moved slowly, and it was a week before his soldiers entered the capital, their bands playing and the local Loyalists cheering heartily as the Redcoats paraded by.

Hamilton, in the meantime, had been sent by Washington into the city to save all the military supplies he could. Hamilton loaded everything that he found on a number of small ships and sent them up the Delaware River where they wouldn't fall into British hands. Then he requisitioned all available blankets and clothing for Washington's ill-provisioned troops, and returned to camp with them. When the British arrived in Philadelphia on the 26th of September they found little of use to them in the city.

Once out of the city and safe in Lancaster, various members of Congress resumed their favorite occupation—criticizing the commander-in-chief. They sent Washington bitter messages, blaming him for his failure to save Philadelphia, the humiliation of their flight, and the General's persistent refusal to meet the British in the field where he could beat the enemy once and for all.

Washington, in an attempt to silence his congressional enemies—for a number of congressmen hated him and wanted to place a general of their own choice in his place—decided to launch a surprise attack on Howe's forces in nearby Germantown.

Washington's plans were carefully made. Just before dawn four columns of American troops were to approach Germantown from four directions and fall upon the sleeping enemy. Unluckily, a heavy fog rolled in late at night when it was too late to halt the attack; the troops were already on the move.

Despite the fog and the ill-trained soldiers at his disposal, Washington might have succeeded in his plan except for General Henry Knox's blunder. This was the same general whom Hamilton had met in Manhattan, at Bunker's Hill, the day when Aaron Burr had saved them all by his act of insubordination. Now Hamilton was with Knox again, temporarily assigned to his staff, when the General's column came upon a large house, just north of Germantown, where several hundred British soldiers had fortified themselves behind stone walls and barricades.

Hamilton and the other junior officers advised the General to have the house surrounded by a few hundred troops, and then to march the main body to Germantown in keeping with Washington's original plan. But General Knox said he would not advance while a body of British soldiers remained in his rear. He ordered a full-scale assault on the fortified position. It took hours to capture the stronghold. By then the noise of the engagement had long since warned the British in Germantown. They were awake and alerted to the danger when the other three American columns attacked just before dawn. By the time Knox joined the principal battle, Howe had rushed up reinforcements and the day was lost. The other three columns had been routed and another retreat was underway. Germantown was the last important battle of the campaign around Philadelphia that year, a campaign which ended as badly as it had begun.

Far to the north, though, American fortunes had improved with stunning swiftness. General Burgoyne, marching south from Canada, had met effective resistance. The British and Hessian troops under his command had no experience in guerrilla warfare. The Americans, on the other hand, were mostly farmers, trappers and hunters. They had lived for years on the edge of a wild, primitive frontier, and they were at home in a campaign that was fought as much in the woods as in the open fields. "Gentleman Johnny" Burgoyne drove his army south, harassed continually by American sharp-shooters; he won indecisive battles, but lost too many soldiers and used up too much ammunition in gaining his victories. Finally, by the middle of October, he found himself far from his base of supplies; his army had been reduced by death and desertion to five thousand men; his ammunition was gone, and he was faced by a force of sixteen thousand Americans.

The British general had no choice. He surrendered his entire army at Saratoga, New York, to General Horatio Gates.

The victory at Saratoga was in many ways the turning point of the Revolutionary War. When the news of the American victory reached Paris, France no longer hesitated. She decided to enter the conflict on the American side, against her old European enemy England. And with the promise of French supplies and loans of French money, with French officers to train the raw American troops, and with the French Fleet to fight the English Fleet and to harass English shipping, the chance of an eventual American victory was brighter than it had ever been before.

To Washington, the news of Gates' victory meant an instant change in war strategy. If some of the troops from Saratoga and the north were immediately transferred south to reinforce his own small army, he could attack Howe and attempt to recapture Philadelphia before winter set in.

But as Washington knew all too well, it wasn't going to be easy to get any troops out of General Gates. Gates was a vain and jealous man. He had long believed that he was a better general than Washington and that he, rather than Washington, should have been named commander-in-chief of the Continental Army. Gates was encouraged and flattered by several unscrupulous members of Congress who hated Washington, and who secretly hoped to replace him with Gates, because once Gates became commander-in-chief, their own power would increase enormously.

Gates was elated by his victory at Saratoga and took it as a final proof that he was a better military man than Washington. To show his contempt for Washington, he sent a message to Congress describing the victory, but sent no message of any kind to his military superior. Washington only learned of Burgoyne's surrender through indirect channels.

This was a towering insult, but with the infinite patience

and restraint that were two of his great virtues, Washington swallowed his pride and kept his temper in check. He forced himself to look at the matter coolly. The essential facts were these: if he sent an ordinary military order to General Gates, requesting the transfer of the desperately needed troops, Gates might well refuse to send them; yet if he *could* get the necessary troops from Gates, Washington knew that he could still strike a great blow against Howe before autumn turned to winter.

Washington decided to send an officer from his staff with a personal message to Gates. The officer would describe the local situation at Philadelphia, and through the use of tact and diplomacy, compel Gates to agree to the transfer of troops. The only question was, which officer should he send on such a delicate mission?

For six months Washington had observed Hamilton, had read what he wrote, had heard what he said in conversation, had learned to respect, admire and trust the courage and judgment of his young aide. Without hesitation he called Hamilton to his tent and explained the mission. Hamilton understood all the dangerous implications in the situation. He was delighted that Washington had so much faith in him.

Responsibility was always pleasing to Hamilton. Nothing brought out his energy and enthusiasm so much as the knowledge that the stakes were high and that he was being called on to perform some action of the utmost gravity and importance. The mission to Gates found Hamilton at his best.

On the 30th of October, 1777, Hamilton started riding northward. Because of British patrols and irregular Loyalist bands he had to take a roundabout route, but he rode so long and so quickly that less than three days later he arrived at Fishkill, New York, more than a hundred and fifty miles away.

In Fishkill, Hamilton stopped and talked with Israel

Putnam, another general from whom Washington wanted to obtain troops for the attack on Howe. Hamilton delivered a message from Washington, inspected the camp, and changed some of Washington's orders, on the basis of what he had seen. General Putnam promised that two of his brigades would be sent south immediately to General Washington.

Then Hamilton rode off the same night and reached Albany two days later. Unshaved, dirty, without sleep, he went straight to General Gates.

The "Hero of Saratoga" received him promptly and listened to the message from Washington, He, Gates, was requested to send three brigades south without delay. These troops, plus General Putnam's two brigades, were sufficient, Washington felt, to ensure the defeat of Howe and the recapture of Philadelphia.

General Gates listened politely, and decided not to obey. Why should he? He was a better military commander than Washington. What victory had Washington won to compare with Saratoga? Why should he, the victor over General Burgoyne, have to give up most of the soldiers under his command? He had friends in Congress. At that very moment they were trying to push through a bill to give him what would be almost an independent army, free of Washington's control. Why *should* he give up his troops?

But Gates didn't say any of this to Hamilton. He offered other reasons why it would be unwise or difficult to send the reinforcements to Washington. New England was still not safe from the British. He needed his troops to protect New England. All the same, he would do his best to comply with Washington's orders. He would send as many men as he could spare. But *not* three brigades.

Hamilton struggled to keep his temper, knowing exactly what thoughts were passing through the general's mind. He sought to persuade Gates, to reason with him. The best he could gain was a promise that one brigade would be sent south.

Hamilton retired and wrote a discouraged letter to Washington, explaining why he had not pressed Gates for more troops. He explained that Gates had great popularity in New England and powerful friends in Congress. He could make no end of trouble if he were pushed too hard. He, Hamilton, had thought it best to settle for one brigade, and to treat the general with kid gloves.

But when Hamilton rode out to inspect the brigade that General Gates had offered to send, he almost danced with rage. He was so angry that he didn't trust his temper. Instead of rushing back to see Gates, he wrote him this short letter, leaving tact and diplomacy out.

> By inquiry I have learned that General Patterson's brigade, which is the one you propose to send, is by far the weakest of the three now here, and does not consist of more than about six hundred rank and file fit for duty. Under these circumstances, I cannot consider it either as compatible with the good of the service or my instructions from his Excellency, General Washington, to consent that that brigade be selected from the three to go to him; but I am under the necessity of desiring, by virtue of my orders from him, that one of the others be substituted instead of this—either General Nixon's or General Glover's—and that you will be pleased to give immediate orders for its embarkation.

Gates was startled by this angry letter from the young lieutenant colonel. It put him in an unpleasant position. Either he agreed to what was demanded, or he openly defied General Washington—and this he was unwilling to do.

The Hero of Saratoga called Hamilton to another meeting. Hamilton found him easier to deal with this time. He would not only send Patterson's brigade, as he had promised to do, but he would send Glover's brigade as well. Hamilton left

General Gates' quarters with the pleasant knowledge that he had brought the rebellious hero to heel.

While in Albany, Hamilton spent an evening with General Philip Schuyler and his family. Schuyler, one of the wealthiest and most powerful men in New York, had been exchanging letters with Hamilton for some time. Their political views were conservative, and very much in agreement. The general, pleased with Hamilton's writings, was even more pleased with his personality and appearance. It was the first time they had met, and a warm friendship was established that night which grew even stronger in the following months and years.

Hamilton not only dined with the general, but with the general's wife and three of his daughters. The second oldest of the Schuyler girls was Elizabeth. Called Eliza or Betsy, she was not a great beauty, though she was charming and pretty, and if Hamilton had been less concerned with his mission, he might have given her more thought.

At any rate, she was certainly worth noticing. Hamilton's friend and fellow aide, Tench Tilghman, had seen her two years before and had been sufficiently impressed to write about Eliza in his diary.

"I was prepossessed," Tilghman wrote, "in favor of this young lady the moment I saw her. A brunette with the most good-natured lively dark eyes that I ever saw. . . . Mrs. Livingston informed me that I was not mistaken . . . for that she was the finest tempered girl in the world."

Elizabeth and Hamilton met that night, and then the young officer was off again; though he had scarcely slept at all for a week, he hurried down to Fishkill. Here, to his astonishment, he found that General Putnam, despite his solemn promise to send two brigades, had not sent a single soldier.

Hamilton, nearly mad with rage, went to George Clinton, the Governor of New York. Though Hamilton and Clinton were to become political rivals a few years later, they were

now on close terms. The governor was extremely understanding. With his help, money was raised to give the soldiers their
back pay—some had refused to march until they received it—
and General Putnam promised that the brigades would move
south.

Then, his mission completed, Hamilton was struck by a
severe illness. He ran a high fever, his body was racked by
excruciating pain, his condition became critical. Governor
Clinton learned of Hamilton's illness and sent his own doctor
to his bedside.

For two weeks, Hamilton was delirious; the doctor gave up
hope for his life. An aide of Clinton's described the last days
of the attack.

"On the 25th in the evening he seemed to all appearances
to be drawing nigh his last, being seized with a coldness in the
extremities, and remained so for the space of two hours, then
survived. . . . On the 27th, in the morning, the coldness came
on again, and increased (he was then cold as high as his
knees) in so much the doctor thought he could not survive;
he remained in this situation for near four hours, after which
the fever abated very much, and from that time on he has
been getting better. The doctor now pronounces him out of
danger."

While Hamilton was sick, a letter came from General
Washington, who had no idea that Hamilton was almost dead.
"I approve entirely," the General wrote, "all of the steps you
have taken; and have only to wish, that the exertions of those
you have had to deal with, had kept pace with your zeal and
good intentions." The letter from Washington must have had
a beneficial effect on the convalescing soldier.

Until December, Hamilton was not strong enough to return south, and when he finally reached Washington's Headquarters he found the army ready to move to winter quarters
at Valley Forge. He also learned that the four brigades had

reached the camp, but only after such delay that it had been too late for Washington to begin his campaign to recapture Philadelphia. Hamilton had done his best and had almost paid with his life, but the exertion and the risk had accomplished nothing.

14

---◆•◆---

A PLAYER OF MANY ROLES

Duricng the war years that followed, Hamilton played many different roles. In the field, he was a brave and trusted officer; in camp, he was the author, with Washington, of orders, letters, and other important papers which the General sent to Congress, the States, the army. And when Washington needed an agent to carry out some delicate mission, perhaps to negotiate with the British for an exchange of prisoners, or to meet with a French admiral to coordinate battle strategy, it was usually Hamilton who was chosen to handle the matter.

Nor was Hamilton idle in his off-duty hours. Letters, political articles, pamphlets, flowed from his pen. His brain was teeming with ideas to strengthen the country, to hasten the end of the war, and to build a new nation once the peace had been secured.

As almost every American knows, the winter of 1778 at Valley Forge was a terrible one for Washington's army. The soldiers were cold, ragged, half-starving. Many of them didn't even have a pair of shoes, so that when they came out of their tents to cross the snow of the encampment they left a trail of bloodstained footprints behind them.

Again and again Washington had Hamilton write letters to Congress, begging for supplies to feed and clothe his sick and wretched soldiers. But Congress delayed, and did almost nothing. The members were more interested in fighting among themselves about petty political questions than they were in improving living conditions for the common soldier.

When he saw how Congress was acting, Hamilton wrote an angry letter to George Clinton, the Governor of New York. What had happened, Hamilton asked rhetorically, to the great men who had formerly been in Congress? Were they dead? Had they deserted the Patriot cause? No, Hamilton informed the Governor, they weren't dead and they hadn't deserted. They had left Congress to serve in the army, or, more frequently, they had returned to their own states to take public office.

"The only remedy," Hamilton wrote, "is to take them out of these employments and return them to the place [Congress] where their presence is infinitely more important."

Here Hamilton had discovered the great weakness that would plague America for the next decade and longer: there was an almost total lack of real national spirit in the country. Too many American leaders preferred to serve at home, in their local governments, than to serve in Congress. Too many of the most talented and able Americans felt far greater loyalty to their own states than they did to Congress and the Confederation. In 1778, Governor Clinton agreed with Hamilton. Ten years later, when Hamilton was leading the fight for a new Constitution and a strong federal government, Governor Clinton of New York would be one of his strongest opponents.

At the very time that American soldiers were suffering so

needlessly at Valley Forge, an event of major importance took place which eventually did much to change the course of the war. France, encouraged by the victory at Saratoga, finally signed a treaty of alliance with the American Government and openly entered the conflict against England.

That same spring, when Washington had secured fresh volunteers and much-needed military supplies, a new and important figure appeared on the scene. He was Frederick William Baron von Steuben, a German general with vast military experience and ability. Benjamin Franklin, one of America's Commissioners to France, had met von Steuben in Paris and had persuaded him to come to America to assist the cause of independence. Von Steuben was one of a number of outstanding Europeans, like the French leader, the Marquis de Lafayette, and the Polish patriot Thaddeus Kosciusko, who served in the American Army with great distinction.

Washington received von Steuben with hearty approval. He appointed the Baron the inspector general of the army, and gave him a task he was ideally suited for—the training of America's inexperienced volunteers. Von Steuben did his job well. After their training under him, the Americans were better soldiers than they had ever been before.

With winter over and French warships reported on the way across the Atlantic to harass the British Fleet, the fortunes of war began to change. The new British commander in Philadelphia, General Henry Clinton, learned of the approaching French ships; he did not dare to keep his troops divided, some in New York, some in Philadelphia. He decided to give up Philadelphia and consolidate his forces in New York. Lacking enough ships to transport his entire army, he prepared, instead, to march overland through New Jersey. Washington's scouts reported the British departure from Philadelphia, and Washington set out from Valley Forge in quick pursuit.

The Americans caught the British Army at Monmouth. In all likelihood the battle would have been a decisive American victory, shortening the war by months or even years, except for the strange behavior of Charles Lee, one of the American generals. His conduct was never satisfactorily explained. Some of his fellow officers believed he was guilty of treason, of deliberately trying to lose the battle. Others said that he was merely an incomparable bungler.

The battle was raging fiercely. Hamilton's friend the Marquis de Lafayette, at the head of an advance column of American troops, was being hotly pressed; major support was needed, and Hamilton rode from the front to see where it was. He found General Lee, who was in immediate command of the battle, advancing with five thousand men, but with no scouts to protect his flanks.

Hamilton checked his horse on a small hill. Looking across the fields he saw a detachment of British cavalry on the left, in a position to fall on Lee's unprotected flank with devastating effect. He spurred to the general, told him the situation, and suggested that an American battalion be sent to the flank. Lee gave his approval, and Hamilton rode off to issue the order.

Then Hamilton hurried back to Washington and reported the incident. Together with the rest of the staff, Washington and Hamilton were soon back at the spot where Lee had last been seen.

It was now a place of wild confusion. General Lee and his soldiers were retreating in complete disorder into the nearby woods, flinging away their arms as though they had been thoroughly beaten and were now flying before a gigantic and victorious host of the enemy.

Yet, unbelievably, there wasn't a single British soldier in sight. What had started the panic was never determined. Washington was furious and relieved Lee of his command. A few days later General Lee was tried by court-martial and disgraced.

With Lee's five thousand men out of the battle at a critical moment, an American triumph was about to become an American disaster. Washington sent Hamilton to summon all possible reserves. Hamilton carried out the order, then galloped to the front, where Lafayette's men were giving ground before the whole British Army.

Hamilton found another officer, Colonel Olney, who was trying to halt the flight of a shattered brigade. Hamilton joined him and they rallied the soldiers. When the British charged the position, thinking to finish off the brigade, the Americans met them with heavy musket fire and cannon shot. As the British fell back in surprise, Hamilton leapt on his horse and led the counterattack. A musket ball hit his horse, the animal stumbled and fell, and Hamilton pitched head-long to the ground.

Luckily the British did not renew their attack at that point and Hamilton was rescued by his soldiers and carried behind the American lines. He learned afterwards that Washington had taken personal direction of the battle and had beaten the British by sundown, though not decisively. And it was an empty victory because the chance to crush General Clinton's army had been lost.

Several weeks later, when Hamilton had recovered from his bruises, Washington sent him on a mission to meet the commander of the French Fleet, Admiral D'Estaing. The admiral had arrived outside New York Harbor with thirteen ships of the line and had anchored off Sandy Hook, bottling up not only a smaller British fleet but the entire British garrison in the city. Hamilton carried with him Washington's plans for coordinating an attack on New York. The American Army was to strike against the city from its nearby encampment in

New Jersey, while the French ships were to sail into the bay, attack the British ships, and spread fear and confusion among the enemy.

Once again, Washington's patience was severely tested. D'Estaing had already decided not to risk his ships in a fight with the British. He met with Hamilton just once. Then he raised anchor and sailed away to Rhode Island, and Washington's chances of retaking New York went with him.

The personal impression that Hamilton made on many important men may be judged by what Admiral D'Estaing wrote a number of months later. In a letter to Washington, on a secret matter, he said of Hamilton, though they had met only once: "I entreat you not to confide the secret to any person, except Colonel Hamilton. His talents and his personal qualities have secured to him forever my esteem, my confidence and my friendship." During the war Hamilton was a friend of most of the European leaders in the American camp—Lafayette, D'Estaing, von Steuben, Admiral Du Portail and Colonel Fleury—and these friendships proved to be lasting ones following the war.

After 1778, most of the major battles of the War of Independence were fought in the south, far from Washington's Headquarters. Until Yorktown, the last battle of the war, Hamilton saw no other military action.

With more and more time on his hands, Hamilton's thoughts turned to the serious financial problems facing the country, problems which Congress had been trying to handle without much success since 1775. During the spring and summer of 1779, Hamilton analyzed these problems carefully, and decided what steps Congress and the separate states could take to improve matters. Then he set down his thoughts in a long letter to General John Sullivan, now a member of Congress from New Hampshire.

The gravest of all problems facing the country, Hamilton said, was inflation. In 1779, a paper dollar, far from being worth a dollar, was actually worth only two cents in coin. At the same time, the price of flour, wool and manufactured goods had gone sky-high.

Yet Congress had to continually buy flour, wool and manufactured goods in order to feed, clothe and arm its soldiers. And, of course, the question was, how much of anything could Congress buy with money that began to lose its value the very day it was printed?

Faith in America's dollar had to be restored, Hamilton said. He proposed a number of steps to be taken to accomplish this.

For one thing, Congress had to be given the power to raise money for itself by levying taxes. Under the Articles of Confederation, Congress didn't have the authority to tax. Only the States could raise money by taxation. To get the money it needed, Congress had to ask the States for it—and then the States gave Congress just as much or as little as they felt like giving.

But, Hamilton said, even if Congress had the power to tax, it could not raise enough money to meet the country's needs. Money had to be raised by other means. The best way would be by foreign loans. Even the largest and richest countries in Europe found it necessary to take out foreign loans when they went to war and needed extra money. Why, then, shouldn't America, weak and poor as she was, do the same?

One further step was needed to halt inflation and restore the value of the American dollar. The wealthy classes in America had to be encouraged to support the country's paper money. "The only plan that can preserve the currency," Hamilton said, "is one that will make it the *immediate* interest of the moneyed men to cooperate with the government in its [the currency's] support."

To interest the moneyed men, Hamilton proposed the formation of a National Bank. Shares in the bank would be sold to private individuals, so that the bank would be owned half by the government and half by the individual shareholders. Profits from the bank's operation would be divided fifty-fifty. And because those profits would depend on a sound American dollar, the moneyed men would do their utmost to see that the value of that dollar rose, instead of allowing it to fall. The moneyed men would benefit in the process, but the country as a whole would eventually benefit even more.

General Sullivan and a few other members of Congress were impressed by Hamilton's ideas. But the letter accomplished nothing at the time. Neither Congress itself nor the States were ready to accept the idea of a National Bank. The individual States did not accept the idea that Congress should be given the power of taxation. These proposals had to wait a dozen years before they were acceptable to the country.

Of Hamilton's most significant suggestions, only the foreign loan was finally adopted. Money was obtained from both France and Spain, and inflation was temporarily slowed. These loans kept America in the war; without them the Confederation would have collapsed and independence would have slipped away.

15

---◆◆◆---

A PLAN FOR THE COUNTRY

Dissatisfied with his life at Headquarters, Hamilton, during the summer of 1779, asked to be relieved of his duties as aide-de-camp. He submitted a request that he be transferred to the south, where there was an active front, and that he be given the command of a battalion there.

Washington never realized how much Hamilton hated the idea of serving as his secretary. He did know that competent battalion commanders were as plentiful as sparrows, while the man who could handle the paper work of an army was a rare bird indeed. Valuing Hamilton so highly, he turned down the request. Hamilton, thwarted in his desire to return to combat, began to harbor a growing resentment against the commander-in-chief. He was more determined than ever to quit his post as secretary, but for a while he did no more about it.

Washington's army spent the winter of 1780 at Morristown. Martha Washington, the General's wife, came north to preside over the General's table, while many rich Patriots, especially those with marriageable daughters, came to Morristown to help enliven the social life of the war-weary officers.

Among the visitors in camp were General Philip Schuyler, his wife, and their daughter, Elizabeth. Eliza and Hamilton now had all the time in the world to be together. They danced, they talked, and a deep attraction grew between them. Hamilton was a dashing officer, popular, known for his daring, and attractive to women. Eliza was pretty, had a slim waist and a trim ankle, and while she was not a brilliant conversationalist or a remarkable beauty, she was charming, intelligent and gracious.

The general watched the growing romance with satisfaction. He had long admired Hamilton, and meeting him again did nothing to lessen his belief that Hamilton had a brilliant future before him. Their political ideas were similar, and the older man saw in his prospective son-in-law a strong ally for future political battles in New York.

That Hamilton loved Eliza there can be no doubt. That he realized the practical advantages such a marriage would bring him, there can be no doubt either. The Schuylers were one of New York's four or five leading families. The general was not only rich—he owned fifty thousand acres around Albany—but he was also a political force in the state. Once allied to the Schuylers, Hamilton's political fortunes, despite his youth, poverty and birth, would improve.

When Hamilton approached the general to ask for his daughter's hand, there was only one small difficulty. The general and his wife were a trifle uneasy because so little was known about Hamilton's background. It was said that he had come to America from the West Indies while still a boy—but what about his parents?

The general undoubtedly asked Hamilton point-blank for a brief family sketch—and Hamilton undoubtedly told him *almost* everything, of his father's aristocratic connections in

Scotland, his mother's French forebears, her early and tragic marriage to the wealthy John Levine—everything except the fact that James and Rachel had never been legally married.

Such a disclosure—had it ever been made—would have ended the marriage plans. The general was far too proud to have allowed his daughter to marry a man who was illegitimate, no matter how brilliant his future might be. So, perfectly clearly, Hamilton did not tell him. And because there was a war, and letters between America and the West Indies were infrequently received, there was no other way for the general to obtain further information. Nor did he, until much later, when the disclosure no longer mattered. In the meantime, that spring, General and Mrs. Schuyler gave their approval and Eliza and Hamilton became engaged, with the wedding scheduled for December.

During the summer of 1780, James Duane, at that time representing New York in the Continental Congress, came from Philadelphia to Morristown to discuss the growing crisis in America with Washington and his generals. Duane, along with John Jay, Robert Livingston and Philip Schuyler, was a leading member of the wealthy and conservative class in New York State. Duane had known Hamilton for a long time and respected his opinions.

In camp, Duane and Hamilton met again. They talked about the innumerable problems besetting Congress and the country, problems which, Duane said, seemed to have no solution. The condition of the country was shocking. Paper money was almost valueless. The army was falling apart through desertions, because there was no food for the soldiers and no money to pay them. When Congress asked the States for money, the requests were ignored.

Hamilton agreed that the situation was grave, but unlike other men with whom Duane had talked, Hamilton said that there were definite measures that could be taken to improve conditions and save the country from ruin. Duane was immediately won over by Hamilton's ideas. Get them down on paper, Duane said, and send them to me in Philadelphia.

Hamilton set himself to the task. Now he was no longer writing as a popular pamphleteer anxious to stir up a controversy or inflame the public; he was writing as a statesman who looks at his country's condition in a dark hour and proposes, in simple, sober terms, the remedies to cure that country's ills.

The opening sentence of his letter to James Duane cut to the heart of the matter. "The fundamental defect is a want of power in Congress," he said. ". . . it has originated from three causes, an excess of the spirit of liberty, which has made the particular States show a jealousy of all power not in their own hands . . . a diffidence in Congress, of their own powers, by which they have been timid and indecisive in their resolutions, constantly making concessions to the States, [and] a want of sufficient means at their disposal to answer the public [needs]. . . ."

Hamilton then went on to answer the common argument that Congress could not act because, under the Articles of Confederation, it was granted no definite powers to act. Congress, Hamilton said, should have assumed those powers. "The public good required that they should have considered themselves as vested with full power *to preserve the public from harm.*"

Then Hamilton said, "But the Confederation itself is defective." A confederation of states was doomed to fail as long as each state in that confederation had complete power over all of its own internal affairs.

Such a confederation—such a country—Hamilton said, would always remain weak. For after all, what makes *any* country strong? Among other things, a country must have control of its own money. "Without certain revenues," Hamilton said, "a government can have no power. That power which holds the purse strings absolutely, must rule." In the present case, the individual states held the purse strings, and Congress, the national government, remained weak. To remedy this defect, he suggested that Congress be granted the permanent authority to raise money by a poll tax, a tax on land, and a tax on commerce.

Hamilton went on to describe what other authority Congress should have, and what authority Congress should not have. It was really a plan for a new government.

Congress, Hamilton wrote to Duane, should have complete authority over questions of trade, finance, war and peace, banks, foreign affairs, and treaties. The individual states should have authority to deal only with matters concerning "the rights of property and life among individuals." In addition, Congress should give up its present attempt to be both a legislature and an executive. A new branch of government was needed, an executive branch, with departments of War, Marine, and Finance. Here, in primitive form, was the beginning of America's cabinet system, a system in which a Secretary of War, a Secretary of the Navy, a Secretary of the Treasury, each served as a department head under the President.

Then, Hamilton said, the war could be won more quickly if the army were reorganized. Enlistments should be made for the duration of the war; the State militias should be disbanded; if enough volunteers did not appear, there should be a national draft. To finance the war, taxes should be raised, money should be borrowed abroad, and a National Bank should be created to stabilize the dollar.

Above all, Hamilton insisted, Congress must be made strong and vigorous, and must be made to *seem* strong and vigorous to the American people. For, he said, "Men are governed by opinion . . . [and] this opinion is as much influenced by appearances as by realities. If a government appears to be confident of its own powers, it is the surest way to inspire the same confidence in others."

The letter to Duane was an amazing document for a man of twenty-three to have written. Hamilton's originality and foresight were astonishing. At the very moment when the States were strongest, he called for a curb on their power. Eventually, their power was curbed. At the very moment when the power of Congress was weakest, he called for that power to be strengthened. Eventually it was strengthened.

Time was needed for the leaders of the country to see the wisdom in many of Hamilton's plans. But even in the autumn of 1780 the letter was circulated by James Duane, and Hamilton became accepted not merely in New York, his own state, but in many other states too, as one of the country's most brilliant and important political thinkers.

16

---◆◆◆---

MARRIAGE—AND A QUARREL

THE summer and autumn of 1780 was another dark period
for America. The country was torn by unrest. In the army,
officers and men complained about bad food, poor equipment
and lack of pay. Washington was under attack from Congress
and the States for failing to win the war, and Hamilton, his
chief aide, came in for his share of public abuse. The French
Fleet had done little against the British Fleet. South Carolina
had been overrun, and General Horatio Gates, the "Hero of
Saratoga," had been sent south to take command. He met
General Cornwallis at Camden.

Camden was one of America's great defeats. The militia
fled at the first charge, and their commanding general fled
even faster—and further. Hamilton, writing to Elizabeth
Schuyler, his fiancée, couldn't keep out a certain note of
malicious satisfaction. General Gates, he said, "seems to know
very little what has become of his army. He showed that age
and the long labors and fatigues of a military life had not in
the least impaired his activity, for in three days and a half he

reached Hillsborough, one hundred and eighty miles from the scene of the action, leaving all his troops to take care of themselves. . . ." So much, Hamilton implied, for the man who had believed himself a better choice for commander-in-chief than George Washington.

Hard on the heels of Camden, there came to light one of the ugliest stories of the Revolutionary War, a story whose last episode Hamilton saw as an eyewitness.

General Washington and his staff had been in Newport, Rhode Island. They were returning south and were a few miles from the vital fort of West Point on the Hudson River, where Washington had planned to spend the night. However, when the General received an invitation to stop at a private house along the way, he accepted the invitation. Hamilton was sent ahead, just before dawn, to explain the delay to the Commanding Officer of West Point, General Benedict Arnold, and to say that General Washington would arrive in time for breakfast.

Benedict Arnold's treason plot had long since been made. He had agreed to betray West Point for a sum of money and a British Army command. The final arrangements had been decided on the day before. The British were to attack West Point as quickly as possible, and after a token resistance, Arnold would surrender the vital fort. Major André, the unfortunate British spy, had left Arnold the previous day, with the plan for the surrender hidden in one of his riding boots.

At dawn, Hamilton greeted General Arnold with the news that the commander-in-chief, accompanied by General Knox and General Lafayette, would soon be arriving at Arnold's home for breakfast. Arnold was secretly delighted. Not only would he deliver West Point to the British, he would deliver General Washington and his entire staff as well.

What Arnold didn't know was that Major André had been

captured and searched, the papers had been found in his boot, and part of the plot revealed. The morning dragged on, but Washington didn't arrive. He had stopped to inspect some fortifications on the way.

Then a messenger came and delivered a letter to General Arnold. The Americans who had captured Major André hadn't realized at first that Arnold was the American traitor. They had sent him a message saying that an English spy had been captured—and Arnold knew the game was up.

Arnold turned pale, asked to be excused, and went to his rooms. He packed hurriedly, sent a message to Hamilton that he was going to cross the river to the fort, then ordered his pretty wife, Peggy, to be called. At the time, and for many years afterwards, no one realized that she was aware of the plot, and had even urged Arnold to commit treason. Arnold told her the news, and she fainted. Without pausing to revive her, Arnold sped out by the back door, mounted a horse, and fled down the bank of the river till he came to the spot where a British sloop, the *Vulture*, was at anchor. He was rowed on board and later taken to England, one of America's great generals, who had sold out his country.

When Washington and his staff arrived at Arnold's home, Hamilton knew nothing of Arnold's flight. Washington went over to the fort to look for Arnold, and while he was gone, the papers taken from Major André were brought in. Hamilton began to read them; as he did, Washington came back from the fort, already feeling uneasy at not finding Arnold. Hamilton handed the General the papers. At first neither of them could believe that Arnold was a traitor. And yet the more they read the clearer it became, until at last they no longer could doubt it.

Washington had trusted Arnold, and had admired him as one of his best generals. Afterwards, Washington spoke of the episode in his usual way, calmly and without excessive bitterness. "Traitors," he said, "are the growth of every country, and in a revolution of the present nature, it is more to be wondered at that the catalogue is so small than that there have been found a few."

Two months later, on the 14th of December, 1780, Alexander Hamilton and Elizabeth Schuyler were married in Albany. Later there was a huge reception in the Schuyler mansion. It was a spectacular affair. The Schuylers and their innumerable relations and friends were there, the women in satin gowns that touched the floor, the men in silk breeches and jackets, white stockings and powdered wigs. Hamilton, of course, had no relatives present, but his officer friends came to Albany, and their uniforms added a dazzling touch to the festivities.

After his marriage, Hamilton should have been content in every way. He loved Eliza, a sweet-tempered girl who worshiped him blindly. Her father, General Philip Schuyler, already admired Hamilton so much that he no longer cared about Hamilton's background; when rumors about Hamilton's birth finally began to circulate in the months that followed, the older man received them with indifference. Hamilton was his hope for the future, his adored son-in-law who could do no wrong. Shortly after the wedding the general wrote to Hamilton:

> You can not, my Dear Sir, be more happy at the connection you have made with my family than I am. Until a Child has made a judicious choice, the heart of a parent is continually in anxiety, but the anxiety vanished in the moment I discovered where you and she had placed your affection.

Besides a dazzling marriage, Hamilton had achieved other successes. He had rich and powerful friends. He had a growing reputation for a knowledge of public affairs and government problems; he was Washington's trusted lieutenant, and sometimes he was called—perhaps by his enemies as well as his friends—"the brains" of the army. Yet with all of this, he was not satisfied. His daily life in the army was becoming an almost unbearable irritation. He hated his work as Washington's secretary. He decided that at whatever cost, he had to get away from his job at Headquarters.

Since the commander-in-chief had already turned down his request for a transfer to combat, Hamilton searched for other avenues of escape. He tried, without Washington's knowledge, to secure a diplomatic post in France. Congress refused to appoint him, selecting, instead, his friend John Laurens.

Balked in this attempt, Hamilton again asked Washington for a command in the field. Again Washington refused. His secretary was invaluable; anyone could command a battalion, only Hamilton could do the work at Headquarters.

Hamilton turned in another direction. The post of adjutant general had become vacant. He asked his friends, General Nathanael Greene and General Lafayette, to help him secure it. They wrote enthusiastic letters on his behalf to Washington. But their efforts were in vain. Washington explained, quite truthfully, that he had nominated another colonel for the vacancy, and that the nomination had already been sent to Congress for approval.

After their wedding, Hamilton and Eliza returned to Washington's Headquarters, where Eliza became one of the young officers' wives superintended by Martha Washington. Hamilton resumed his duties as the General's secretary, but he was more determined than ever to escape.

Another avenue appeared to open. After many months, Congress had finally agreed to put into law some of Hamilton's plans for improving the government and the conduct of the war. One change was to replace the Committee on Finance with a single official, the Financier. The question was, who had enough knowledge of economic matters to fill the post?

General John Sullivan and James Duane, remembering Hamilton's ideas and suggestions, tried to push the twenty-four-year-old officer's name through Congress. But congressional sentiment leaned to Robert Morris—another admirer of Hamilton, but a fine choice in his own right. Morris was finally selected as Congressional Financier, and Hamilton was frustrated again.

By now, Hamilton believed, quite wrongly, that Washington was deliberately and secretly trying to prevent his leaving Headquarters, and so he made up his mind to pick a quarrel with Washington, and afterwards, to resign his post as aide-de-camp.

In the middle of February, 1781, an opportunity presented itself. Hamilton was running downstairs at Headquarters with an important order in his hand. On the stairs he passed General Washington, who said, "I would like to speak to you, Colonel Hamilton."

Hamilton said, "I will wait upon you immediately, sir." He ran down the stairs to the lower floor and gave the order to Tench Tilghman with instructions to insure its delivery. As he started back, he met General Lafayette in the hall. They talked for several minutes on a military matter. Then Hamilton excused himself quickly and ran back upstairs.

Washington was standing at the top of the stairs, purple with anger. "Colonel Hamilton," he roared, "you have kept me waiting here more than ten minutes. I must point out to you, sir, that you treat me with disrespect."

"I am not aware of it," Hamilton said in an icy voice. "But since you think it right to tell me so—we part!"

Washington's eyebrows went up. He stared. Then, still boiling, he said, "All right, sir, if that is your choice."

And each turned on his heel in a fury and stalked away.

Washington got over his anger almost at once. With monumental forbearance, he sent a message of conciliation to Hamilton. But his young aide spurned it—he was determined to get away from his job as secretary no matter what happened. A second time Washington offered to make peace. A second time Hamilton politely but coldly refused. That made the breach final. Hamilton submitted his resignation as the General's aide-de-camp, and Washington had no choice but to accept it. Hamilton retired to Albany, an exile from the war.

17

THE WAR'S END

On the same day that he submitted his resignation, Hamilton wrote a letter to Robert Morris, the new Congressional Financier, in Philadelphia. Though Robert Morris had been given the job that Hamilton had wanted for himself, he admired Morris and bore him no ill-will. Hamilton's letter was filled with suggestions for Morris, and for the country.

America, Hamilton said, was in worse trouble than ever. Had France not loaned and given money to the States during the past years, they would never have been able to continue the war against England.

Now more money was needed, but this time France, in financial straits herself, could make no further loans. Spain and Holland were no better off than France. Where, then, was the money to come from?

Hamilton returned to his favorite plan—a National Bank. Only a National Bank, whose stock would pay a generous dividend, could help solve the country's financial crisis. Why? Because nothing else would induce the rich men of the country to loan their private funds to the government. Rich men—like all men, Hamilton said—were motivated largely by self-interest, cynical as that might sound. Make it clear to the rich that they would benefit by loaning money to the government and they would do it. Otherwise, they would not.

Then Hamilton turned to his other favorite theme—the weakness of Congress. The Articles of Confederation, loosely binding the States together, were useless. They had to be changed—the government had to be completely reorganized, overhauled. But how to go about it? Hamilton had an answer.

"It has ever been my opinion," he wrote, "that Congress ought to have complete sovereignty in all but the mere municipal law of each State; and I wish to see a convention of all the States, with full power to alter and amend . . . the present futile and senseless Confederation."

Here was something new—the idea that delegates from all the States should gather in a convention, to draft a constitution for the ailing country. It was the first time that such a convention had been suggested, the first time that a strong Federal Constitution was foreseen. Hamilton's letter sounded the first note in the struggle for a powerful central government, and for the as yet unwritten Constitution of the United States.

Hamilton, retiring to Albany, did not give up his dream of military glory. It was his obsession and it continued to haunt him. His father-in-law, General Schuyler, tried to persuade him to enter Congress, assuring him that his appointment would be approved without difficulty. Hamilton turned down the suggestion. He still dreamed of war, and in July of 1781, General Washington, ignoring Hamilton's previous conduct, finally granted him a field command. On the 31st of the month, Hamilton took over an infantry battalion composed of two New York regiments.

Washington planned that summer to attack General Clinton's forces in New York with the help of the French, but two things forced him to change his strategy. The first thing was that General Clinton received unexpected reinforcements, making New York all but impregnable. The second thing was that in the south, General Lafayette's small army had been unable to prevent General Cornwallis from ravaging huge sections of Virginia, and it soon became necessary to rush help to him.

In short order Washington marched his army south to Virginia, moving with such speed and secrecy that neither General Clinton in New York nor General Cornwallis in Virginia realized what he had done. Meanwhile the French Fleet, under Admiral de Grasse, sailed south to Chesapeake Bay to challenge the British ships protecting General Cornwallis' army.

General Clinton now made a grave blunder. He still believed that Washington meant to attack him in New York, and he ordered General Cornwallis to send all possible British troops north from Virginia to help defend the city. Cornwallis obeyed, hoping that the British Fleet would still be able to protect his weakened army.

Hardly had the British troops sailed north, when Admiral de Grasse and the French Fleet appeared in Chesapeake Bay. They engaged the British men-of-war, and in a five-day battle, beat them badly. The British remnants fled north to New York, and a French troop convoy soon landed in Virginia and joined forces with Washington's Army.

Cornwallis perceived that he was in a trap. He was surrounded on a narrow strip of land, with the French warships in control of the waters behind him, and with a combined army of American and French troops in front of him.

Hamilton saw that Cornwallis would probably be beaten, and that once he surrendered, the war would be practically over. He had gotten his command just in time—a few weeks later would have been too late.

There were two key fortifications that had to be attacked first. Hamilton, serving under his old friend General Lafayette, was stunned to hear that one fortification was to be attacked by French forces, the other by American troops under a Colonel Barber.

Hamilton rushed to Lafayette. *He* had every right to command the attack, not Colonel Barber. *He* was the Officer of the Day. The honor of leading the charge belonged to *him*—

But, Lafayette explained, he could do nothing to change the order. The order had come directly from General Washington at Headquarters.

Hamilton, almost blind with frustration, believed that Washington, out of spite and enmity, had deliberately plotted to keep him from his chance at glory. He scribbled a hasty note to Washington, claiming the attack as his privilege. Washington, patient as always, changed the order just in time, and Hamilton was put in charge of the American troops.

The attack began at six o'clock in the evening. The French charged on the left, Hamilton's men on the right. As it grew dark, bursts of gunfire lit up the field. With Hamilton was his old friend and comrade-in-arms John Laurens, in command of eighty men.

Hamilton was in his glory. He raced at the head of his troops, indifferent to the firing of cannon and musket. He came to a deep ditch and leapt into it. He disappeared, and for a moment it was thought that he had been cut down. Seconds later he was standing on the other side, urging his men to attack. The fortification fell that same hour, with Hamilton leading his men in the final charge, his sword waving above his head.

A few days later, on the 19th of October, 1781, General

Cornwallis surrendered his entire army at Yorktown. Though a peace treaty with England was not signed until two years later, the American War of Independence had finally been won.

18

A NEW CAREER

Like many other young officers, Hamilton retired from active service after the victory at Yorktown. He returned to his father-in-law's house in Albany where Eliza soon gave birth to Philip, the first of their eight children.

Life for Hamilton was pleasant enough in Albany. Eliza was delighted to have him home, and she was a good-natured and affectionate wife. Hamilton's father-in-law was kindness itself. He said that nothing was too good for Eliza, Hamilton, and their infant son.

General Schuyler again urged Hamilton to enter politics. Though many political jobs paid poorly, the general assured Hamilton that he need not concern himself about money; he had only to make known his family's needs, and the general would gladly find the means to satisfy them.

This did not suit Hamilton at all. His pride could not tolerate the idea of accepting any more help from the general than necessary. Hamilton decided that he had to find a way

125

to earn his living, so that he could start to support his wife and child.

By now he knew that his talents fitted him ideally for the law. So he invited his former college roommate, Robert Troup, who was already a lawyer, to come to Albany to help him with his legal studies. Hamilton applied himself to his lawbooks with his usual zeal. By July he had passed the State examination and was licensed to practice in New York State.

In the meantime, he had been asked by Robert Morris, the Congressional Financier, to take the job of Receiver of Taxes for New York. Hamilton accepted the job reluctantly, more to help the struggling Financier than for any other reason. He did not believe that taxes could be effectively raised for the government as long as the separate States would not cooperate fully. And usually they would not cooperate at all.

In New York, for instance, Governor George Clinton had by now become an enemy of Congress. He didn't want to see a penny leave his state for the use of the national government in Philadelphia. After several months of wasted effort, and with almost no money raised, Hamilton in utter disgust resigned his job as Receiver of Taxes.

Perhaps more clearly than any other man in the country, Hamilton understood why America was drifting toward disaster. His pen was never still. In newspaper articles, pamphlets, private letters, he kept expressing again and again his fundamental ideas: the country was weak and growing weaker; the Articles of Confederation had to be radically changed or discarded completely; a strong federal government had to be formed, or the Thirteen States would fall into anarchy, bankruptcy, ruin.

Other men might put loyalty to their states ahead of loyalty to their country, but Hamilton, born in the West Indies, felt no such fanatical devotion to New York. His loyalty was to his adopted country, not to any particular section of it. The Thirteen jealous, quarreling States, however, were not yet ready to follow Hamilton's lead. Conditions would have to grow even worse before his views could be accepted.

Finally, though, Hamilton did yield to the pleas of his father-in-law, and entered the political arena. He was appointed a delegate to Congress, and in November, 1782, left Eliza and his infant son and journeyed south to Philadelphia.

He served as a congressman for almost a year, but accomplished little. He did, however, meet James Madison, a young delegate from Virginia, whose views at the time were very similar to his own. He and Madison formed a temporary political alliance that was to prove invaluable three years later during the fight for the Federal Constitution.

The Continental Congress, in which Hamilton served, was a powerless and pitiful organization. Nobody heeded it. Few men served in it willingly. Several states didn't even bother to send a single delegate. The same forum which had framed the Declaration of Independence only six years before was now without friends, honor, or respect.

Within the country there was grave unrest and it would mount higher, year by year. In 1782 and 1783, the army, both officers and men, was in a mood close to rebellion. They rightfully wanted their back pay, and refused to give up their arms and return to their homes until they had received it. And Congress, unable to raise money through taxes, and receiving no money from the States, was unable to pay the country's soldiers.

Shocking events followed. On one occasion, Washington himself had to calm a mutiny of officers. On another, the building in Philadelphia where Congress sat was surrounded by a mob of three hundred armed soldiers, which threatened the delegates with violence if their demands for pay were not met.

Hamilton protested to Governor Dickinson and insisted that the local militia be called out, but the governor refused. During the ensuing panic, one of America's most disgraceful episodes took place. In the middle of the night the delegates to Congress were forced to flee from Philadelphia to escape the wrath of their own countrymen, not stopping till they had reached Princeton, forty-five miles away. Here they finally found the situation more secure, and remained in Princeton for the rest of the term.

When Hamilton left Princeton for Albany in July, 1783, congressional prestige had fallen to a new low. Seven States did not have a single delegate in attendance. Although the army revolt had been quieted, the nation, as Hamilton knew, was in growing peril. But he was powerless at the moment to effect a change.

In November, 1783, after a peace treaty was signed with England, the British garrison finally evacuated New York City. Hamilton left Albany several days later. Returning to the city, he opened his first law office at 57 Wall Street, and here, for the next three years, he remained in private practice.

Many of New York's leading lawyers had been Loyalists, and the State refused to let them practice now. This allowed many young lawyers to rise quickly to the top of their profession. Within a short time Hamilton, his friend Robert Troup, his political associates, John Jay and Rufus King, and a retired army major, Aaron Burr, were the leading lawyers of the city. By 1786, Hamilton had only one rival. He and Burr were pre-eminent in New York's law courts. At first, their rivalry was a friendly one.

Hamilton's reputation as a lawyer was firmly established by a single case that was tried early in his career. New York

State at the time was filled with Patriots bent on revenge. During the war they had often suffered great hardships, while the Loyalists in the city and the State, under the protection of the occupying British Army, had lived in luxury. Now the Patriots wanted to get some of their own back. The New York legislature, heeding their demands, passed punitive laws against the Loyalists. These laws not only deprived many Loyalists of their rights and property, they did so in open violation of the terms of the peace treaty which America had just signed with England.

One of the punitive laws was called the Trespass Act. Under its terms, any New York citizen whose property had been occupied during the war by a Loyalist could now sue that Loyalist for damages. When such cases were tried, the courtroom was packed with Patriots. Often they were the poorest and most vicious elements in the brawling city, and they crowded the benches, waiting for a verdict which would inflict heavy fines on another of their hated enemies. It took courage to defend a Loyalist under such conditions, and few of the city's lawyers accepted Loyalist clients. Hamilton, however, did accept them, and his reputation was established by his defense of a Loyalist named Benjamin Waddington.

The case appeared to be open and shut, and Hamilton was called a fool for undertaking Waddington's defense. The facts were not in dispute. A widow named Elizabeth Rutgers was the owner of a brewery on New York's Maiden Lane. In September, 1776, when General Howe's forces had occupied the city, Mrs. Rutgers, a staunch Patriot, had fled from New York with General Washington's retreating army. The British had taken over her brewery and operated it for themselves until June, 1778, at which time they had given Waddington a license to run the brewery, charging him an annual rent of one hundred pounds.

When the British, under the recent peace treaty, had finally left New York in 1783, Mrs. Rutgers regained possession of her property. The brewery had suffered no damages while Waddington had operated it. Nevertheless, under the provisions of the Trespass Act, Mrs. Rutgers sued Waddington for heavy damages.

Feelings over the case ran high in the city. The Patriot majority whipped itself into a hot fury over the "poor Patriot widow" who had suffered so much because of her support of the Revolutionary cause. The city mobs rallied behind her and demonstrated in the streets. Her brief was accepted by three eminent lawyers, among them, Robert Troup.

Hamilton had never believed in mob rule. Years before, he and Troup had risked injury at the hands of a city mob in order to save their college president, the arch-Loyalist Dr. Myles Cooper. Now the mob was forcing the State to enact unjust laws to satisfy its hate and greed, and Hamilton instinctively arose to combat what he felt was an attack on individual liberty.

He based the defense of Waddington on two major points. The first was a narrow, legalistic one. Hamilton said that the brewery had been abandoned by Mrs. Rutgers, and then had been taken over by General Howe for the benefit of his army, "as by the laws, customs and usages of nations in time of war he lawfully might do," and that General Howe had later licensed the brewery to Benjamin Waddington "under the protection of said army."

The second point of the defense was more far-reaching. Here, Hamilton attacked the Trespass Act itself. He began by saying that the act violated certain provisions of the peace treaty recently signed with England, provisions which protected Loyalists like Waddington from just such claims as that of Mrs. Rutgers. Hamilton went further. He took the unpopular position that a treaty made by Congress was the supreme law of the land, and that when any local or state laws conflicted with that treaty, they were improper laws and their force was invalid. Congress, Hamilton said, had the full right, power and authority to sign treaties which were completely binding on the individual states, and the states could not justly or legally enact laws which violated those treaties.

James Duane, long Hamilton's colse friend, was then Mayor of New York, and he sat in judgment on the case. His view of the question was close to Hamilton's, but he also knew that Patriot sentiment was violently hot, and that if he dismissed Mrs. Rutgers' suit and failed to award her damages, the resulting disturbances might be hard to put down.

Duane's decision was a curious compromise. On Hamilton's second point, his major one, Duane concurred. A treaty, Duane said, entered into by Congress, was indeed the law of the land, and "we are clearly of [the] opinion that no state in this union can alter or abridge . . . the . . . articles of the treaty."

But, Duane went on, in Mrs. Rutgers' suit against Waddington there were special circumstances that had to be considered, and special legal points that had to be weighed. Duane apparently weighed them—and remembering the mobs outside in the streets, and gazing at the rough, angry faces inside the courtroom, judged that certain damages had to be paid to Mrs. Rutgers, the Patriot widow, by Benjamin Waddington, the Loyalist merchant.

Though Waddington had to make a settlement, Hamilton's reasoning and his conduct of the defense won him wide notice and approval. New clients flocked to him, and soon he had all the legal work that he could possibly handle.

The Trespass Act itself continued to be a state law in New York until 1788, when Hamilton's political party won control of the legislature and repealed all laws that were in conflict with the peace treaty of 1783. Only then did the persecutions and the bitter hatred against the Loyalists begin to subside, and some of the scars left by the war begin to heal.

19

---•◆•---

THE GREAT CONVENTION

ALTHOUGH the years 1783–1786 were prosperous years for
Hamilton, they were disastrous years for the country. By 1786,
foreign trade was almost nonexistent. Manufacturing was at
a standstill. America's farmers were deeply in debt, and had
no apparent way of escaping their indebtedness. The country
owed money to France which it could not repay. Inflation in
the Thirteen States was rampant. To solve these problems, the
States simply printed more paper money—and the inflation
which already gripped the country became that much worse.

In 1786, Hamilton was elected a member of the Assembly,
New York State's lower house. He was by now a recognized
leader among those who wished to see the Articles of Confederation replaced by a Federal Constitution—hence, these
men began to be called "Federalists." Hamilton and his political allies, then and in later years, tended to represent the
large landowners, the merchants and the bankers.

The Assembly in New York was controlled by Hamilton's
political foes, led by Governor George Clinton. Clinton and

his associates represented the small farmers and tradesmen, and the working classes. They began to call themselves "Anti-Federalists," and then, after a time, "Republicans." The political struggles of the next few years, both in New York and throughout the country, were between these two emerging political parties—the Federalists and the Republicans.

Hardly had Hamilton taken his seat in the New York Assembly, when he heard a piece of news that he considered vital. James Madison—soon to be a leading Republican, but at that time a leading Federalist—had succeeded in having a resolution passed in the important Virginia legislature, calling for a convention of delegates to meet in Annapolis, Maryland, "to study United States trade and commerce, in order to improve them."

This was the opening that Hamilton had been waiting for. Once such a convention met, there was no reason for the delegates to limit themselves to a study of "trade and commerce." They could begin the work of making the nation strong and preventing it from fragmenting itself forever into a number of separate, puny, and impoverished nations.

In September, 1786, Hamilton traveled to Maryland to serve as one of New York's delegates to the Annapolis Convention. Besides New York, only Virginia, Delaware, Pennsylvania and New Jersey sent delegates. The other states, controlled by enemies of the Federalists, viewed the Convention with suspicion. That so few states were represented was a disappointment to Hamilton. But he resigned himself to a slow, patient course. He offered a resolution calling for another convention, to be held in May, 1787, in Philadelphia, with delegates representing *all Thirteen States* in attendance. That convention would be called for the purpose of discussing, Hamilton proposed, "a uniform system of commerce, and for such other purposes as the situation of public affairs may be found to require."

The resolution was passed. Thus at Annapolis, Hamilton laid the groundwork for the great Constitutional Convention that was to transform thirteen weak and ineffective states into a new nation.

Although conditions were growing steadily worse in all parts of the country, there was still tremendous opposition to Hamilton and the Federalists, and to any suggestion they made that the Articles of Confederation should be replaced by a strong Federal Constitution. Several of the States, bitterly jealous of their power and authority, would probably have refused even to send delegates to Philadelphia had not a frightening event taken place in western Massachusetts, early in 1787.

The farmers of western Massachusetts were deeply in debt. The Massachusetts legislature, controlled by the bankers and merchants of Boston and the other eastern cities, passed laws which only increased the farmers' indebtedness. The farmers' cattle were seized, their farms were foreclosed, and often they themselves were thrown into debtor's prison.

The farmers of western Massachusetts revolted. Led by Daniel Shays, a Revolutionary War captain, they swarmed across the countryside in armed bands, forcing the local courts to close, burning public records, and threatening local officials. Then they marched eastward toward Boston, to compel the legislature to alter the laws. The state militia was called out, and the farmers were defeated in a pitched battle. Forced to flee and hide, they were hunted down and treated severely.

The news of Shays' Rebellion sent out waves of shock in every direction. If a revolt could erupt in Massachusetts, it could erupt in any of the other states. Under the threat of rebellion and even of civil war, the enemies of the Federalists were forced to yield some ground. With caution, fear, and great reluctance, all thirteen state legislatures agreed to send delegates to the proposed convention.

On the second Monday in May, 1787, fifty-five delegates from the Thirteen States met in Philadelphia. Most of them were Federalists. Washington was the presiding officer. Most of them understood, as Hamilton had understood for almost ten years, that if the country were to survive, the Articles of Confederation would have to be discarded and a new Federal Constitution written to replace it. Although the delegates were not there for that specific purpose, they soon forgot all other work. The drafting of a Constitution became their self-appointed task.

The first proposal offered to the Convention was the so-called Virginia Plan. It called for a legislature composed of two houses, the equivalent of our Senate and House of Representatives, and an executive officer, the equivalent of our President, who would be appointed by the legislature. The legislature would be empowered to use force against any state when necessary, and would be able to veto any law of any state which violated a federal law. Each state would have a number of representatives in the legislature, based on the size of its population.

This plan, the smaller and less populous states felt, would favor the larger states. So a second proposal was offered to the Convention, the so-called New Jersey Plan. Under the New Jersey Plan, there would be only one house in the legislature instead of two, and every state would have the same number of representatives, regardless of its population. This plan clearly favored the smaller states.

The Convention divided over the two plans, and for days and weeks speeches were made and compromises suggested. Hamilton offered two amendments, both of which were soundly defeated. Until the very last days of the Convention, he did only one other thing. On the 18th of June he delivered a carefully reasoned, five-hour speech outlining his beliefs of what the new government should be.

Hamilton's plan was modeled on the British form of government, as he freely admitted. Two houses (like the English House of Lords and Commons) were called for. Members of the upper house would be elected for life. There would be an executive, also elected for life. Hamilton also stated with candor that he saw little value in the separate states, and believed in reducing their power as much as possible. He believed that the country would grow and prosper more surely as its citizens came to think of themselves as Americans, rather than as Virginians, New Yorkers, or Pennsylvanians.

Hamilton's plan was strongly nationalistic—to that extent, it had merit. It also would have established an aristocratic form of government, and to that extent it was totally unsuited to America. When Hamilton had finished his speech there was absolute silence for several moments. Then, without anyone attempting to answer any of his carefully reasoned arguments, the delegates went on to a fresh subject—as though the speech had never been made.

Later, in private, a number of delegates congratulated Hamilton. His conservative views were very close to their own. But they could not back his views publicly. For the delegates knew that the writing of a new constitution was only the first part of their task; the second, and by far the hardest part, would be to get at least nine of the states to ratify that constitution once it was written. For the country as a whole did not really want a new constitution or a strong central government. In every state there were powerful men who would oppose with all their strength whatever constitution was written in Philadelphia. To have accepted Hamilton's ultraconservative views would have been to doom the ratification of the Constitution in advance. And so, many of the delegates ignored their own personal beliefs and Hamilton's, and tried to write a document which would be "democratic" enough to be accepted by a majority of their countrymen.

Shortly after making his speech, Hamilton left the Convention and did not return to Philadelphia until the writing of the Constitution was almost finished. On the surface, it was a strange thing for Hamilton to do. Ever since 1779, he had insisted that a new constitution was needed to save the country, yet when it came time to write that constitution, he walked out of the proceedings.

Some historians have said that after his speech was ignored, Hamilton left the Convention in a fit of temper. Others have said that he never had any ability to compromise; since his own views were too conservative, he decided to ignore the work that was being done.

Neither charge is true. Though Hamilton's temper was occasionally hasty, he never lost it in Philadelphia, in 1787. Nor was he incapable of compromise, as events were to prove a few months later.

Hamilton's conduct had a much more obvious explanation. He was a practical man in many respects, and he knew that he had little to contribute to the Convention's discussions at that moment. Rather than sit idly in Philadelphia, he returned to New York where he had close and powerful political allies, and where he could use his influence to gain fresh support for whatever document was being written by the delegates.

During his absence in New York, George Washington wrote him several letters to keep him informed. By this time Hamilton and Washington had long since forgotten their quarrel. In the years following the war, Washington's respect for Hamilton's abilities had grown enormously. They were both politically conservative, and usually were in complete agreement as to what was best for the country.

"I *almost* despair of seeing a favorable issue to the proceedings of the Convention," Washington wrote to Hamilton. "The men who oppose a strong and energetic government are in my opinion narrow-minded politicians, or are under the influence of local views." Then Washington added, "I am sorry you went away; I wish you were back. The crisis is equally important and alarming and no opposition under such circumstances should discourage exertions, till the signature is fixed."

On the 2nd of September, Hamilton reappeared at the Convention. The Constitution was almost finished. Hamilton had known in advance that it would not incorporate many features he would have preferred, but when he read the document, his objections were few and mild. Then he proved that he was capable of compromise, that he was, in the highest meaning of the word, a statesman. He roundly condemned the delegates "who say they will vote against the report because they cannot get all parts in it to please them." He said he would accept and support *any* system that would promise to save America from the dangers with which she was threatened.

Hamilton made an eloquent speech before the Convention when the Constitution was presented to it. He asked every delegate to sign it, no matter how he felt about it or how he voted on any particular provision of it. A unanimous approval was necessary to impress the people at home, he said. "A few characters of consequence," he added, "by opposing or even refusing to sign the Constitution, might do infinite mischief." What choice, he insisted, could there be between a plan, however imperfect, on the one hand, and anarchy and ruin on the other?

Hamilton signed the Constitution for New York. His two fellow delegates, both Republicans, had long since left the

Convention, refusing to have any share in proceedings which they opposed completely.

Three other delegates who were present, Randolph and Mason of Virginia, and Gerry of Massachusetts, also did not sign the Constitution.

Then the Convention disbanded and the delegates went home to their states, where the fight began at once over ratification. It was a fight in which Hamilton led, and in many ways it was the most important undertaking of his life.

20

---·•·---

THE FEDERALIST ESSAYS

THE struggle over the Constitution of the United States was furious and bitter. Opposition to ratification was strong, often violent, in all Thirteen States.

In order to ratify, each state was obliged to elect by popular vote a special ratifying convention. The conventions of nine states had to vote in favor of the Constitution before it could become the law of the land. At the beginning, the chance of winning nine states seemed doubtful.

One of the keys to the struggle proved to be *The Federalist,* a series of political essays written between October, 1787, and August, 1788. The idea for *The Federalist* was probably Hamilton's. He wrote the first essay, and at least two-thirds of the more than eighty that followed. John Jay, in New York, wrote five, and James Madison, in Virginia, wrote the remainder. The essays were all signed with the pen name "Publius," for the authors had agreed to remain anonymous. Although the entire series was addressed "To the People of the State of New York," the various essays were widely read in the other

States and influenced many citizens in favor of the Constitution.

The Federalist was written to defend the Constitution against its critics, and to encourage its adoption by the various state conventions. Hamilton began the first essay by pointing out the importance of the coming decision. Addressing himself to his fellow New Yorkers, he said, ". . . you are called upon to deliberate on a new Constitution for the United States of America. The subject speaks its own importance. . . . It has been frequently remarked that it seems to have been reserved to the people of this country, by their conduct and example, to decide the important question, whether societies of men are really capable or not of establishing good government from reflection and choice, or whether they are forever destined to depend for their political constitutions on accident and force. If there be any truth in the remark, the crisis at which we are arrived may be regarded as the era in which that decision is to be made; and a wrong election of the part which we shall act may, in this view, deserve to be considered as the general misfortune of mankind."

The next four essays of *The Federalist,* written by John Jay, stressed the importance of a strong United States, capable of defending itself against foreign aggression. Then Hamilton wrote four essays in which he pointed out the civil disorder that would follow if the Constitution were not adopted—ending with a reminder of Shays' Rebellion which had taken place so recently in Massachusetts.

The most famous single essay of the series, No. 10, was written by Madison—whose views within two or three years, under the influence of his political mentor, Thomas Jefferson, were to change completely. Madison outlined the ways in which the Constitution would protect the rights of minorities against the will of the majority. He said that while it was true that every class and every group inevitably voted for its own interest, the American Consitution contained built-in guarantees that would safeguard the weaker party in political, economic and civil disputes.

Then Hamilton took up the burden. He wrote that the country would flourish financially under the Constitution, and that all classes would share in the prosperity.

He and Madison wrote on and on, at a furious pace. Hamilton wrote many of the essays in whatever time he could snatch between legal cases. For while he was writing *The Federalist,* he was also practicing law in New York in order to support Eliza and their growing family.

Clause by clause and section by section, he and Madison examined the Constitution; Hamilton took the lead here, answering objections that had already been raised, discussing disputed clauses, and doing it so well that in later years many judges of the Supreme Court would turn back to *The Federalist* in order to interpret some part of the Constitution.

In the last essay, Hamilton closed out his case. "I never expect to see a perfect work from imperfect man. . . ." he wrote. "The compacts which are to embrace thirteen distinct States in a common bond of amity and union, must as necessarily be a compromise of as many dissimilar interests and inclinations. How can perfection spring from such materials?" Yet the basic point remained undisturbed—the basic point he had made at the Constitutional Convention: Something was better than nothing, a very imperfect Constitution was better than none, anything was better than weakness, anarchy, disunion.

Thomas Jefferson, soon to be the country's leading Republican, and Hamilton's political rival, read *The Federalist* essays in France, where he was serving as America's envoy. Since the essays were all signed "Publius," he didn't realize that they were more the work of Hamilton than of his political protégé, Madison. He wrote to Madison that he found

The Federalist essays "the best commentary on the principles of government that ever was written." It was almost the last kind word he had for anything that Hamilton wrote or did.

Washington also read *The Federalist,* and wrote to Hamilton, ". . . the perusal of the political papers under the signature of Publius has afforded me great satisfaction. . . . I have seen no other [work] so well calculated . . . to produce conviction in an unbiased mind, as the *production* of your *triumvirate.*"

While *The Federalist* essays appeared and spread their influence, the various states elected their special ratifying conventions. Delaware, New Jersey and Pennsylvania ratified the Constitution before the end of 1787, and Georgia and Connecticut ratified the Constitution early in 1788. These states had been counted on by Hamilton and the Federalists. The real struggles would be fought in the four populous states of Massachusetts, South Carolina, Virginia, and New York where the opposition was particularly strong. Hamilton led the fight in New York, and kept in constant touch with Madison, who led the fight in Virginia.

In New York, of the delegates elected in April, 1788, to the special ratifying convention, only nineteen were Federalists, while forty-six were opposed to ratification. At the outset the odds appeared too long for Hamilton, but he realized that he had several advantages which did not immediately appear on the surface.

Among the forty-six delegates who were opposed to ratification, there were a number who might be willing to accept the Constitution if they were guaranteed that a "Bill of Rights" would eventually be added to it. And while only nineteen delegates were outright Federalists, their numbers included many of the most important, able, and respected men in the state. Besides Hamilton, their acknowledged leader, there was John Jay, soon to be the first Chief Justice of the United States Supreme Court; there was also Richard Low, Isaac Roosevelt, Robert R. Livingston, James Duane, and General Philip Schuyler, men who had held innumerable political and military posts in the past, and whose opinions now carried considerable weight among all but their bitterest opponents.

In addition, Hamilton took heart because he understood the difficult problems that confronted Governor George Clinton, the leader of the Anti-Federalists. An early vote in New York would surely turn down ratification; but, Hamilton believed, Governor Clinton would not be happy to see that happen. For if nine other states should then approve the Constitution, after New York had turned it down, reprisals might be made against New York for having taken such action. Also, New York City was solidly Federalist; if the State failed to ratify the Constitution, the City might then secede from the rest of the State, and join the Union on its own, cutting off the State from much of its trade and revenue.

On the other hand, if New York *did* ratify the Constitution quickly, it would help to decide the other wavering states, and this would ensure the very acceptance of the Constitution to which Governor Clinton was so strongly opposed.

Faced with this dilemma, the governor decided to proceed as slowly as possible. He wanted to see what the other states did first. And this was exactly what Hamilton had hoped for. The longer the delay before the New York Convention met, the more *The Federalist* essays could exert their influence among the uncertain New York delegates; the longer the delay, the more chance that nine of the other states would vote for ratification, and this too would influence the uncertain delegates.

Finally, Governor Clinton agreed to convene the New York Convention in Poughkeepsie, on the 17th of June. By the time the first delegates began to arrive in the sleepy Hudson River town, Massachusetts, Maryland and South Carolina had voted for ratification. South Carolina was the eighth state to do so. Now everything hinged on New Hampshire and Virginia, since nothing at all could be hoped for from stubborn Rhode Island or North Carolina, and little could be hoped for from New York until at least a ninth state, and perhaps even a tenth, had already ratified the Constitution.

General Schuyler came down to Poughkeepsie from his home in Albany, and he was already waiting in the capital when Hamilton, Chancellor Livingston and John Jay arrived from New York City. They had ridden north on the Albany Post Road, through deep forests and along the rolling hills that bordered the majestic river. Hamilton had found the journey a pleasant relaxation from work, and an excellent means of gathering his strength for the struggle ahead. He reached Poughkeepsie in a confident frame of mind that was shared by few of the Federalists, and certainly not by his father-in-law, General Schuyler.

Governor Clinton, the general reported, was sure of defeating ratification. And why not? He had the votes in his pocket, didn't he? And Poughkeepsie was the governor's town, the seat of his power. His large country house, on the outskirts, was the meeting place for all the Anti-Federalists. They wined and dined there, and many of them had comfortable lodgings as well. On the other hand, the general complained, he and the Federalists had to put up at a wretched inn, accept the worst possible sleeping accommodations, and eat food that not even a dog should be asked to swallow.

But Hamilton's confidence soon restored the spirits of the general and the other Federalists. The final vote, he said, would be decided by debate and reason, not by fine food and drink and a few soft feather beds. Inconveniences they could put up with—as long as they won.

Fortunately for the bodily comfort of the little band of Federalists, they did not have to remain long at Van Kleek's tavern on the Upper Landing Road. An invitation arrived from Henry Livingston to make use of his house during the convention, and the Federalists accepted the invitation unanimously.

Hamilton liked to be comfortable as well as the next man. When they had all moved into the Livingston house, he expressed his satisfaction with their new arrangements, saying, "It has the advantage of privacy. Here we can hold conference nightly with no fear of eavesdropping. Moreover, to get a bath at Van Kleek's is as easy as making love to Clinton."

Certainly Hamilton did not approach the greatest struggle of his life with a heavy heart.

21

THE FIGHT
IN POUGHKEEPSIE

HAMILTON's strategy at Poughkeepsie was to avoid an early vote at all costs, and to keep the Convention in session as long as possible. He had established a horse-express between Virginia and Poughkeepsie, and another between New Hampshire and Poughkeepsie, and he hoped to hear by courier at any time that either of those two states had finally voted for ratification; this news, he felt sure, would influence some of the Anti-Federalist delegates to accept the Constitution.

He also hoped to induce some of the Anti-Federalists to change their votes through his own powers of argument and persuasion. He believed, quite rightly, that no man in the opposing camp, certainly not the governor, and not even the governor's ablest lieutenants, Robert Yates, John Lansing, or the brilliant speaker, Melancton Smith, could successfully stand up to him in a prolonged debate. Hamilton's plan was to keep talking, to reply point by point to every objection the opposition could raise to the Constitution, and to whittle away at the opposition's strength through every skill known to the art of the public speaker.

The New York Convention began its work on the 17th of June in the Poughkeepsie courthouse. The room was packed with local citizens, most of them Anti-Federalist supporters of Governor Clinton, whose election as President of the Convention they applauded loudly.

Hamilton was on his feet at the Convention almost every day. Sometimes he spoke briefly, sometimes he spoke at length. Sometimes he spoke softly, sometimes he spoke with a voice of steel and with eyes cold and burning. By turns he charmed and soothed, he awed and frightened his listeners. He moved them to laughter, he moved them to tears.

His principal opponent in the debates was Melancton Smith, who raised a variety of objections to the Constitution and the idea of a strong federal government. One by one, Hamilton demolished his objections.

Melancton Smith said that under the proposed Constitution, the rich and powerful would run the country—and rich and powerful men were almost invariably vicious. Hamilton replied, "Experience has by no means justified us in the supposition that there is more virtue in one class of men than in another." Then he added slyly, "Look through the rich and the poor of *this* community, the learned and the ignorant— where does virtue predominate?"

Melancton Smith said that under the Constitution there would be little true democracy in the country. He cited the cities of ancient Greece as models of true democracy. Hamilton drew on his vast knowledge of history for his reply. "The ancient democracies," he said, "in which the people themselves deliberated, never possessed . . . good government. Their very character was tyranny . . . when they assembled, the field of debate presented an ungovernable mob . . . incapable of deliberation."

Melancton Smith shifted his ground. If the Constitution were ratified, he said, he feared that the power of the States would be fatally undermined. Hamilton rose quickly to his feet again. His small, erect figure held every eye in the room. He knew that on this vital point he had to reassure the Anti-Federalist delegates or not one of their number would vote for ratification.

"The state governments," he said, "possess inherent advantages which will ever give them an influence and ascendancy over the national government, and will forever preclude the possibility of federal encroachment." He went on at great length to explain why this was inevitably so, and after he had finished, several of the Anti-Federalist delegates indicated that they were now leaning to the Federalist side.

The Convention had been sitting for a week when, on the 24th of June, word was brought to Hamilton that a courier had been seen on the turnpike, riding toward the town from the north.

Hamilton slipped from his seat, went outside the courthouse, and mounted a horse. He galloped north and met the courier on the outskirts of the town.

The courier, covered with dust, reined in his horse. He handed a letter to Hamilton, who broke the seal with trembling fingers. Inside was a terse message. New Hampshire had voted for ratification. The United States of America had finally come into being.

A few minutes later, when Hamilton announced the news to the Convention, the small band of Federalists cheered lustily, while a heavy silence fell over the ranks of the Anti-Federalists. But Hamilton spent little time rejoicing. He feared the outcome in Virginia. Unless Virginia ratified the

Constitution, New York would also refuse to ratify, and without New York the Union would soon collapse and the Thirteen States would go their separate ways.

Hamilton immediately sent a letter off to Madison, telling him the good news about New Hampshire, but adding, "We eagerly await further intelligence from you, as our chance of success depends on you. There are some slight symptoms of relaxation in some of the leaders, which authorizes a gleam of hope if you do well, but certainly I think not otherwise."

Hamilton had good reason to fear the outcome in Virginia. Leading the Anti-Federalists in that state was Patrick Henry, perhaps the greatest orator of his time. Allied with him was a majority of the Virginia delegates. Although Thomas Jefferson was not then in Virginia—he was serving as the American Minister to France—his influence in his home state was enormous, and it was known that his approval of the Constitution was at best lukewarm.

Though few in number, the Federalists in Virginia, however, like the Federalists in New York, were outstanding men. James Madison led them, supported by Governor John Randolph, and by a brilliant young lawyer, one day to be a famous Chief Justice of the United States Supreme Court, John Marshall. And more important than any of these was the one man whose influence alone might tip the balance—George Washington. In Virginia particularly his word was held in wide esteem. Hamilton knew that without Washington the cause was hopeless—but that Washington stood wholeheartedly behind the new Constitution.

Early in July another courier raced into Poughkeepsie. He carried a message to Hamilton from James Madison. Virginia had voted for ratification. Now it was up to Hamilton to make the victory complete.

But victory was not to come quickly or easily in New York. The Anti-Federalists fought on. They realized that their own state stood almost alone, and so they offered a compromise. Let the Constitution be changed in certain respects and *then* they would vote for ratification.

Hamilton didn't know how to reply to this proposal. He sped a letter to Madison, asking his advice. Madison replied that he must yield to no compromise. The Constitution would have to be accepted by New York in its entirety and forever—or rejected.

The debate raged on bitterly through the end of June and into the middle of July. Maneuver was met by maneuver, argument by counterargument. "Let us take care," Hamilton exhorted at one point, "not to oppose the whole country!" But the Anti-Federalists remained strong. Though Hamilton had won over some of the delegates, Clinton's party was still in the majority.

On the 25th of July, the Convention came to the critical vote. A proposal by the Anti-Federalists had been offered which called for qualified adoption of the Constitution. Under the proposal, New York would have had the right to withdraw from the Union after a number of years, if the Amendments to the Constitution—the future Bill of Rights— did not meet New York's exact specifications. The voting began. Hamilton, weary to exhaustion, knowing his forces were still outnumbered, tried to appear cheerful and confident, though inwardly he felt that he was a beaten man.

As the voting proceeded, Melancton Smith rose to his feet. He made a brief speech—and the stunned delegates listened in silence. He had been won over by the arguments of the Federalists, he said. The matter was clear, he felt. New York *had* to accept the Constitution, and accept it without any conditions.

Other delegates followed Melancton Smith's lead. The final vote went against the proposal, 28–31.

Hamilton rushed forward a motion of his own, a motion

calling for unqualified adoption of the Constitution. His new support held firm. Hamilton's motion carried. By the slim margin of 30–27, New York voted to enter the Union, and the United States of America was a reality at last.

A few days later there was a great celebration in New York City. Church bells were rung, and there was a huge parade through the city's streets. Prominent in the parade was a wooden replica of a frigate, which had been built by the city's carpenters. It was twenty-seven feet long and had a fully equipped hull and rigging. It was named *Hamilton*. The sailmakers of the city had built another ship, and that "sailed" in the parade too. It was called *Constitution*. As the two ships went by, the crowds cheered wildly. It was probably Hamilton's hour of greatest personal popularity, but all too soon, the hour was gone.

22

---◆◆◆---

SECRETARY
OF THE TREASURY

On April 30, 1789, George Washington took the oath of office on a Wall Street balcony in New York City, and became the first President of the United States. He did not want the office. Writing to Hamilton previously, he had said, "It is my great and sole desire to live and die, in peace and retirement, on my own farm." But Hamilton and many others convinced him that the new nation needed him, and finally Washington agreed to accept the Presidency if that was the will of his countrymen. Soon after, he was elected President unanimously by the members of the electoral college.

Washington's Vice-President was John Adams of Massachusetts. Washington appointed Thomas Jefferson of Virginia his Secretary of State and had him recalled from France, where he was still serving as the American Minister. Washington appointed his staff officer, General Henry Knox of

Massachusetts, his Secretary of War, and Edmund Randolph, the former Governor of Virginia, his Attorney-General.

One more cabinet post, Secretary of the Treasury, remained to be filled. It was the most important cabinet post of all. During the following months and years, the Secretary of the Treasury would have to set up an entirely new system to solve the country's financial difficulties. If he failed, the infant government would go bankrupt, would lose all power, and the Thirteen States would inevitably drift into disunion.

Washington asked Robert Morris, the former Congressional Financier, to take the post, but Morris declined. He had long since had enough of the government's financial woes. He suggested Hamilton as the man best qualified, and Washington readily accepted his suggestion. By then, Washington thought Hamilton very nearly the ablest man in the country, and he relied heavily on Hamilton's theories and opinions. He asked Hamilton to join his cabinet and Hamilton accepted the post of Secretary of the Treasury, becoming, at the age of thirty-two, one of the most powerful men in America.

When Hamilton first took office he was immediately faced with a gigantic problem. It was a problem left over from the past. During the war, both the national government and the States had been forced to borrow huge sums of money. These sums were still owed. What exactly, Congress now asked Hamilton, should be done about these debts? How should they be repaid? And could some of them—say, the debts of the national government—be paid, and others—say, the debts of the States—be forgotten completely?

Hamilton's answer was firm and clear: all the debts would have to be repaid. For the time being, though, he allowed the question of the States' debts to be put aside. In the first of his "Great Reports," "The First Report on the Public Credit," he dealt primarily with the debts of the national government. When he offered this report to Congress, it provoked a storm. Since it opposed the views of Jefferson and Madison, it marked the beginning of what was soon to become an ever-widening gulf between them and Hamilton.

Hamilton began by writing that the debt of the United States was the price the country had paid for its liberty, and that it was nothing less than a national debt of honor, which, like all debts of honor, had to be met. In addition, the public credit of a country was judged exactly as the private credit of an individual. If an individual honored his debts, he was afterwards respected and trusted. If he did not, he was held up to scorn and ridicule and could hardly expect to be trusted again. Exactly the same conditions were true, Hamilton said, for a country. And so, all of the debts of the national government would have to be paid.

In January, 1790, Hamilton announced to the House of Representatives that he had a plan ready to deal with the national debt, and he offered to deliver it in person to the House.

A fight immediately occurred in the House over Hamilton's appearing there in person. Many members feared that Hamilton's ability as a speaker would unduly influence the House in favor of Hamilton's plan. So a resolution was introduced, and passed, that the report should be submitted in writing. And from that time to this, no cabinet member has ever appeared in person to present his proposals or plans to the members of Congress.

Hamilton's report was submitted to the House in writing. The debate on it was long and sharp. Madison, now a Representative from Virginia, offered a compromise, which was defeated. Hamilton's plan was then approved. Funds were voted to pay the interest on the public debt, and more funds voted to reduce that debt.

With the question of the national debt settled, Hamilton

attacked the much more difficult problem of the old war debts of the States. Hamilton's proposal was simple—and violently opposed. The debts of the States, Hamilton said, should be "assumed"—or taken over—by the federal government. Jefferson and Madison were opposed, and before the fight was over, Hamilton, Jefferson and Madison had been called all sorts of vicious and insulting names. Such were the political habits and customs of the time.

The fight over the question of "assumption" was far more bitter than the fight over the national debt. In April, the critical vote was taken in the House, and Hamilton's proposal was defeated, 31–29.

Apparently the debts of the States were not to be taken over by the federal government, and a major part of Hamilton's financial plan was to be tossed into the discard pile.

But now Hamilton engaged in some behind-the-scenes political maneuvering. One of the questions confronting Congress and disturbing the country was where the permanent capital of the United States should be located. New York City was the temporary capital, but this location suited few of the States. Hamilton first approached Robert Morris, of Pennsylvania, and offered to make Philadelphia the capital, in exchange for several of Pennsylvania's votes when a new bill of "assumption" should be offered to Congress.

While Morris was consulting some of his fellow Pennsylvanians, Hamilton approached Jefferson. They struck a bargain over the dinner table: some of Virginia's votes were to be switched to support "assumption"; in exchange, the capital would be temporarily located in Philadelphia (to satisfy Robert Morris), and then permanently located in Georgetown, Virginia, on the banks of the Potomac River.

Years later, Jefferson attempted to explain away his share in the bargain, saying that he had known little about "assumption" at the time, since he had only recently returned from France, and that Hamilton had hoodwinked him into making the "deal." But Jefferson's memory grew dim on certain points as he grew older, and his explanation is contradicted by letters he wrote at the time explaining his conduct.

At any rate, the capital was soon moved to Philadelphia, and then, in 1800, to its present site at Washington, D.C.; in Congress, "assumption" was reintroduced, and passed; the debts of the States became merged with the national debt, and another part of Hamilton's plan to make the nation strong and prosperous had been realized.

When the federal government moved to Philadelphia in 1790, Hamilton found a house outside the city, where he and Eliza and their growing family were to live for the next five years.

Toward the end of 1790, Hamilton proposed another measure to strengthen the country's finances. On the 14th of December, he placed before the House of Representatives a "Supplemental Report," in which he outlined in full his plan for a National Bank.

Eleven years before, in 1779, Hamilton had written his famous letter to General Sullivan calling for a National Bank, a letter in which he explained the benefits that the country would enjoy from the operation of such a bank. Hamilton's National Bank in 1790 was essentially the same Bank he had proposed to General Sullivan. It differed only in detail.

Hamilton's plan for a Bank caused a tremendous explosion. The Republicans under Jefferson were bitterly opposed to it. They said that the Bank would benefit merchants, bankers and speculators. This the Bank did. They said that the Bank would harm and perhaps ruin the small farmer and the poorer classes, the men who made up the backbone of the country. This the Bank did not do. For it greatly stabilized the nation's monetary affairs at a most critical period, and it eventually helped to create a strong and prosperous United States—a country in which millions of small farmers and workers were able to live in modest comfort, if not in great wealth and luxury.

But the Republicans' main attack on the Bank was made on different grounds. The Bank, they said, was unconstitutional. Hamilton, of course, denied this. What happened then was something that no one could have foreseen. A debate began on the Constitution itself. How was the Constitution to be interpreted? What powers did the President really have? What kind of laws could Congress pass, without violating the Constitution?

Jefferson's position was that the Constitution had to be followed almost to the letter. Unless some particular power was authorized by the Constitution, that power did not belong to the President, or, as in the case of the Bank, to the House of Representatives. This "strict" interpretation would have severely limited the powers of Congress and the President; it would have greatly weakened the federal government because it would have severely restricted the activities of the federal government. This is what Jefferson and the Republicans wished to see happen.

Hamilton's position was that if the Constitution did not specifically *prohibit* the President or Congress from taking certain actions, or from using certain powers, then those actions and powers were probably constitutional. On these grounds, the debate over the Bank raged on until the 8th of February, 1791. That day the House voted on a Bill to approve Hamilton's plan for a National Bank. The vote was 39–20 in favor of the Bank.

But Hamilton's victory was still not assured. Washington had to sign the bill before it would become the law—and now

Washington hesitated. The great protest against the Bank had given him grave doubts. Was the Bank unconstitutional? He asked his Attorney-General, Edmund Randolph, for an opinion. Unconstitutional, said Randolph. Washington then asked his Secretary of State. Unconstitutional, said Jefferson.

More uncertain than ever, Washington asked Hamilton for an additional opinion. Hamilton threw himself into the matter with all of his fiery energy. He studied the reasonings of Randolph and of Jefferson, then sat up the entire night answering their arguments. Of all the letters and pamphlets which he wrote during his life, few had a more lasting effect than the letter which he sent to Washington.

The reasonings of a great lawyer on a subtle legal question are not easy to follow in detail. What Hamilton said, in general, was this. First, the "strict" interpreters of the Constitution, like Randolph and Jefferson, were wrong when they said that the United States Government possessed only such powers as were specifically granted in the Constitution. On the contrary, Hamilton said, any government, by its very nature, possesses certain powers which it can only be deprived of by specific laws. In addition, the Constitution contained a clause permitting Congress to enact certain laws which were "necessary and proper" to the welfare of the country. The proposed law to authorize a National Bank was clearly "necessary and proper" to the welfare of the United States. Finally, Hamilton asked, "Does the proposed measure abridge a pre-existing right of any State or individual? If it does not, there is a strong presumption in favor of its constitutionality."

Washington read Hamilton's opinion, and his doubts were settled. He signed the bill into law, and the National Bank was formed not long afterward.

Hamilton's victory not only assured the United States of a stable economy for years to come, it allowed Congress and the President, from that day to this, to assume wide powers and authority that are not specifically granted in the Constitution. Were both Jefferson and Hamilton living today, Jefferson could hardly approve of the way the powers of the President and Congress have grown, whereas Hamilton would undoubtedly think that the nation had acted wisely in following his liberal interpretation of the Constitution.

23

POLITICAL STRUGGLES

Between 1790 and 1795, Hamilton was at the height of his political power. Washington, though a Federalist in outlook, did not take part in partisan politics. Hamilton became the recognized leader of the Federalists, and the Federalists held the reins of government in Philadelphia.

Hamilton already had made numerous political enemies and would continue to make more. He was envied for his tremendous abilities, and detested for the influence he wielded. Most of his enemies were in the ranks of the Republicans, but some of them were members of his own party.

In certain ways Hamilton was not a clever politician. He did not understand how to keep a political party together. Sometimes, when a soft word or a bit of flattery might have served, he neglected to offer the soft word or refused to flatter. Sometimes, when a political plum should have gone to X, he allowed it to go to Y.

The first major setback that Hamilton received came in

New York, in 1791. It was a particularly irritating setback, and quite typically, he brought it on himself.

Hamilton's father-in-law, General Philip Schuyler, had already served a term as United States Senator. In 1791 he was nominated for a new term. The state legislature in New York elected senators then, and since the Federalists controlled the legislature, Hamilton assumed that the general would have no difficulty being re-elected.

Much to Hamilton's surprise and dismay, the general was not re-elected. The Livingston clan, previously loyal supporters of Hamilton, felt they had been neglected. One of their members, by *this* time, should have been made a senator. To revenge themselves on Hamilton for his neglect, they threw their support to a young man with political ambitions, Aaron Burr. Burr was duly elected. General Schuyler retired to Albany, and Burr went to Philadelphia as a senator, where he began to make a name for himself.

Hamilton watched Burr's activities with great uneasiness. He knew Burr well, since they had both practiced law in New York for a number of years, often taking opposite sides of a case. Part of Hamilton's uneasiness must have come at the moment he realized that Burr was a threat to his own political control in New York.

But part of his uneasiness came from a deep conviction about Burr's character. He knew that Burr had a brilliant mind. He also believed that Burr was unscrupulous, a man utterly without principles.

The very next year there was an election in the state for governor. John Jay was the Federalist candidate. Two men were considered possibilities as the Republican candidate. One was Aaron Burr. The other was Hamilton's political foe of ten years, Governor George Clinton.

In a personal letter, Hamilton discussed the two men:

Mr. Clinton's success I should think very unfortunate. . . . But still, Mr. C. [Clinton] is a man . . . as far as I know, of probity. I fear the other gentleman is unprincipled, both as a public and a private man. . . . In fact, I take it, he is for or against nothing, but as it suits his interest or his ambition. He is determined, as I conceive, to make his way to be the head of the popular party, and to climb . . . to the highest honors of the State, or as much higher as circumstances may permit. Embarrassed . . . with an extravagant family, bold, enterprising, and intriguing, I am mistaken if it be not his object to play the game of confusion, and I feel it a religious duty to oppose his career.

Hamilton, then, considered Burr an adventurer and an opportunist, a man to be defeated at all costs. Soon his views became known to Burr, and it wasn't long before the two men hated each other bitterly.

However, the two chief political rivals of the period were not Hamilton and Burr, but Hamilton and Jefferson. Many things divided them. There was an honest and profound difference in their political beliefs. Hamilton believed in a strong national government; Jefferson believed in a weak one. Hamilton believed that the country would benefit if the bankers and merchants were prosperous; Jefferson believed that the country would benefit if the small, middle-class farmers were prosperous. They clashed in their views about America's future. Hamilton foresaw a great industrial and manufacturing nation; Jefferson foresaw a strong agricultural nation. They clashed in their social views. Hamilton distrusted all but the wealthier classes; Jefferson distrusted all but the rural inhabitants, saying of the industrial worker, "The mobs of the great city add so much strength to the support of pure government, as sores do to the strength of the human body."

Both men were ambitious and enjoyed the use of power.

Each saw in the other a great rival and an obstacle to power. But of the two, Jefferson's hatred and animosity were far the stronger. Hamilton saved his hatred for Burr.

Antagonism between Hamilton and Jefferson grew stronger as the months passed. Defeated on the question of the National Bank, Jefferson declared Hamilton his enemy. They began to clash in cabinet meetings. They began to quarrel in the newspapers, as they fought for public support. Hamilton wrote pamphlets which Jefferson answered through his fellow Virginian, James Madison, and through others in the Republican ranks.

Washington's re-election in 1792 did nothing to calm the storm. Hamilton continued to be the most powerful member of the cabinet. He intruded into matters that were clearly the concern of the Secretary of State. Jefferson justly resented the intrusion. But by then his hatred was almost pathological. His attacks against Hamilton were savage, and brought little credit to an otherwise noble reputation.

The "Giles Resolutions" give some idea of the bitter personal and party rivalry that existed at the time. William Giles was a Representative from Virginia, and a friend of Jefferson's. In February, 1793, he placed nine resolutions before the House of Representatives. The resolutions were a personal attack on Hamilton, made for political reasons. They were made at Jefferson's insistence, to discredit and ruin Hamilton.

The resolutions accused Hamilton, among other things, of a wanton disregard of the public interest, of violating an Act of Congress, and of disobeying certain instructions of the President. The resolutions said that Hamilton had seriously mismanaged treasury funds, and demanded an immediate and complete accounting of all of Hamilton's many financial activities as Secretary of the Treasury.

This demand was made on the 27th of February. Congress

was scheduled to adjourn in March, not to meet again until September. Giles' strategy—really Jefferson's—was plain. Hamilton, his enemy thought, would not have time to make an accounting before Congress adjourned; the charges would remain unanswered until September, and in the meantime, all summer long Hamilton would be forced to live under the darkest clouds of suspicion which he could do nothing to dispel.

But the plan failed. Hamilton worked around the clock, slept when he could, ate hasty meals and sped back to his desk again. To the surprise of friend and foe alike, a full accounting of the complete operation of the Treasury was placed before the House within twelve days. Following a vicious debate, the resolutions condemning Hamilton were overwhelmingly defeated.

Jefferson later denied any connection with the resolutions. But a copy exists in his own handwriting, proving that he wrote the resolutions for Giles—except that, instead of nine resolutions, there were originally ten. The tenth resolution had been too strong even for Giles' stomach, though, and he had refused to place it before Congress. It resolved "that the Secretary of the Treasury has been guilty of maladministration in the duties of his office, and should, in the opinion of Congress, be removed from his office by the President of the United States."

Apparently Jefferson was willing to go to almost any lengths to see Hamilton driven from power.

One other example of Jefferson's almost insane hatred should be noticed. In August of the same year there was a great epidemic of yellow fever in Philadelphia. Eliza Hamilton had a mild case and quickly recovered. But Hamilton's case was much worse. Worn out with overwork, he fell seriously ill. He was thought to be dying, because he had the worst form of the disease, and almost no one with his symptoms recovered.

Hamilton's schoolboy friend, "Neddy" Stevens, was now a doctor in Philadelphia. Ned was called in, after Hamilton had been treated for several days by another doctor. Ned Stevens changed the treatment, and to everyone's surprise, Hamilton recovered. Many others were not so lucky. Over four thousand people in Philadelphia died of yellow fever that summer.

At the time, Jefferson wrote to James Madison about their rival, Hamilton:

> Hamilton is ill of the fever as is said. He had two physicians out at his house the night before last. His family think him in danger, and he puts himself so by his excessive alarm. He had been miserable several days before from a firm persuasion he should catch it. A man as timid as he is on the water, as timid on horseback, as timid in sickness, would be a phenomenon if the courage of which he had the reputation in military matters were genuine.

There are truly few more dismal spectacles than a great man blinded to the virtues of a rival by jealousy and hatred.

24

DECLINING YEARS

Hamilton's last years were filled with bitterness and strife. In 1794, defeated at every turn, Jefferson resigned from Washington's cabinet and retired to Monticello, his famous home in Virginia. But before he left the capital, he instigated a new congressional investigation into Hamilton's treasury operations, an investigation which dragged on for more than a year without discrediting Hamilton in any way. Finally, Hamilton, wearied by the continual assaults of the Republicans, weakened by sickness and overwork, and assured that his financial plans and policies had set the new nation on its feet, resigned from Washington's cabinet in 1795, never to hold public office again.

There were also private reasons for his resignation. Eliza had suffered a serious miscarriage, and needed care and attention while she recovered her health. They had five children. Philip, the oldest, was thirteen, John, the youngest, was two, and Hamilton had to earn more money to support them. As Secretary of the Treasury, his salary had been three thousand dollars a year. Before that, in the 1780's, as a lawyer in New York, he had earned considerably more, so that for six years in the capital he had been sacrificing the welfare of his family to the welfare of his country. Now he knew that he had to make provision for his family's future.

In 1795, after a brief stay in Albany, Hamilton and Eliza moved into a small house in New York City, at 56 Pine Street. They later changed houses several times, finally settling at 24 Broadway, where they remained until 1802. Then they moved into a house outside the city which Hamilton called "The Grange" and which he designed himself.

Hamilton was a poor man when he resigned as Secretary of the Treasury. Though he was often accused by the Republicans of making large personal profits out of his government dealings, there was not an ounce of truth in the slanders. During his years in Philadelphia he often had to borrow trifling sums, twenty or thirty dollars, in order to meet his monthly expenses. "I am not worth [more than] five hundred dollars," he wrote to a friend when he resigned from the Treasury. "My slender fortune and the best years of my life have been devoted to the service of my adopted country; a rising family hath its claims."

Talleyrand, the great French diplomat, was in America during the 1790's, having been driven into temporary exile across the Atlantic by the French Revolution. He and Hamilton became friends; they admired one another's abilities. Much later, Talleyrand said of Hamilton, "I consider Napoleon, Pitt and Hamilton as the three greatest men of our age, and if I had to choose between the three, I would unhesitatingly give the first place to Hamilton."

Talleyrand also had another remark to make about Hamilton. One evening in New York, on the way to a party, he happened to stroll past Hamilton's law office, which was nothing more than a little room on the ground floor of his house. The room was lighted by candles. Talleyrand looked through the window and saw his small, thin, energetic friend bending over the desk, law papers strewn about, his hand moving swiftly and surely across a sheet of paper. Talleyrand went on to his party, where he was heard to say with surprise, "I have just come from viewing a man who had made the fortune of his country, but [who] now is working all night in order to support his family." Talleyrand, accustomed to a different standard of official conduct, did not understand how the treasurer of a country could have left office without first putting a good part of the treasury into his own pockets.

Hamilton's nonpolitical friends were pleased to learn that he had returned to private life. They knew that he was very nearly impoverished. But they also knew that, unlike Aaron Burr, who charged the highest legal fees, Hamilton usually asked very little from his clients. And so they wondered how he would ever become rich and secure.

Hamilton's college roommate, Robert Troup, had practiced law in New York without ever having entered politics. Troup was now prosperous, and willingly advanced Hamilton several large amounts of money to help him meet previous loans which Hamilton had been forced to make while serving as Secretary of the Treasury.

Once, in speaking to Hamilton, Troup said in a joking manner, "I sincerely hope . . . that you may by some fortunate . . . event acquire the means of perfect independence in spite of all your efforts to be poor. I have often said that your friends would be obliged to bury you at their own expense." Troup's joking words proved more accurate than he could have imagined.

Another friend of Hamilton's, James McHenry, a fellow aide-de-camp on Washington's staff, wrote to Hamilton from his comfortable home in Baltimore.

I have built houses, I have cultivated fields, I have planned gardens, I have planted trees, I have written little essays, I have made poetry once a year to please my wife, at times got children and at all times thought myself happy. Why cannot you do the same, for after all if a man is only to acquire fame or distinctions by continued privations and abuse I would incline to prefer a life of privacy and little pleasures.

Hamilton believed that he was going to retire from public affairs, live a quiet life, and enjoy "the little pleasures" of a private citizen. But he was far too energetic to remain on the sidelines. Within a month after his resignation from the Cabinet, he was offering advice to Washington and other officials in Philadelphia, advice which was eagerly sought and gratefully accepted. Hamilton became the adviser to many men in his party, and his actual influence remained enormous.

In 1796, after serving two terms as President, Washington retired to his farm in Virginia, opening the way for other men to seek the country's highest office. Although their power was declining, the Federalists were still stronger than the Republicans. Their two leading candidates were John Adams of Massachusetts and Charles C. Pinckney of South Carolina. Adams had never liked Washington or Hamilton, and Hamilton had never liked Adams. In the early part of the campaign, Hamilton supported Pinckney, and even though Adams won the election, he never forgave Hamilton. Before long, President Adams had another grievance against Hamilton, and a much stronger one.

Between 1796 and 1800, Hamilton practiced law in New York, and although he was without public office, he continued to have an important hand in running the government—a fact which President Adams did not discover for three years. When Adams did learn the truth, the break between him and Hamilton became complete.

What happened was this. Several members of Adams' Cabinet were either close personal friends of Hamilton, or were his former political associates. When Adams wanted their advice, they first consulted Hamilton in New York— without telling Adams what they were doing. So Hamilton gave them *his* opinions, and the Cabinet members subsequently passed those opinions on to Adams as if they were really their own. For three years then, Adams, without realizing it, was being guided by Hamilton. When he finally discovered what had been going on behind his back, Adams' rage at Hamilton was gigantic, and nothing could soften it.

The Presidential election of 1800 was the last one in which Hamilton played an important part. It did two things to Hamilton. It broke his political power and it called on him to make one of the most unusual decisions that ever faced an American politician.

In 1800 the Federalists were in danger for the first time of losing the Presidency. Their strength was sinking, the strength of the Republicans was on the rise. Their party was already badly divided by the public quarrels between Adams and Hamilton. Adams was a candidate for re-election, Jefferson was his strong Republican opponent. Then, at a time when the Federalists had to unite as never before, Hamilton helped to split his own party so completely that it never was a truly united party again.

Hamilton's blunder was an inexcusable one for an experienced politician to have made. He wrote a pamphlet highly critical of Adams, and signed his own name to it. The pamphlet was privately printed, and circulated among those leaders whom Hamilton considered "trustworthy." But far too many copies were distributed for the pamphlet to have remained a secret, and indeed, a copy "mysteriously" fell into the hands of Republican Aaron Burr before the ink was fairly dry on the press.

Burr, by then, was not only Hamilton's rival for control of New York, he was also a figure of prominence on the national scene. Burr smiled with delight, and had the pamphlet re-printed widely in Republican newspapers. The Federalists were horrified. All their dirty linen was exposed to the full view of the country. The Republicans were overjoyed. The election, they were sure, was now safely in their hands.

The Republicans were right. When the votes in the electoral college were counted, Adams, the Federalist candi-date for President, had sixty-five; Pinckney, the Federalist candidate for Vice-President, had sixty-four; while the Re-publican candidate for President, Jefferson, had seventy-three, and the Republican candidate for Vice-President, Aaron Burr, had seventy-three also.

Thus the Federalists had lost both offices and the Republi-cans had won them—and yet, because of a defect in the Constitution, Jefferson was still not President. It was true that the men who had voted for Jefferson and Burr had *meant* Jefferson to be President and Burr Vice-President, but their wishes were of no importance. At that time, the Constitution said only that when two candidates had the same number of electoral votes, another and final election between them had to be held in the House of Representatives. There, each state had one vote. And in 1800, since the Federalists still had control of the House of Representatives, it was the Federalists who would decide which of the two Republicans, Jefferson or Burr, would become the next President.

For Hamilton, the choice was clear. There were few men in public life whom he liked less than Jefferson—but one was Aaron Burr. Burr, Hamilton had said eight years before, was a man without principles. There was no limit to which he might not go to benefit himself, whether or not he harmed the country at the same time.

Vote for Jefferson, he told the Federalists. Between the two, there can only be one choice. Vote for Jefferson.

The vote was unbelievably close. Most of the Federalists hated Jefferson, but felt little enmity for Burr. And so, many of them voted for Burr, despite Hamilton's persuasion, his thunderings, his pleas. So far had Hamilton's power slipped away.

The votes of nine states were needed to win, and on the first ballot, Jefferson had eight, Burr had six, and two states were tied, their delegates equally divided.

A stalemate developed. Hamilton continued to struggle. He wrote to Senator Bayard of Delaware; he wrote to him again. Delaware switched its vote to Jefferson.

And so, in 1800, Hamilton's old rival, Thomas Jefferson, was elected President of the United States. And Aaron Burr, the man Hamilton never trusted, the man whose later career included a trial on charges of treason, was kept out of the most important office in the land.

25

———◆———

LAST MEETING WITH BURR

Though Hamilton's power was broken and his national influence greatly reduced after his fight with Adams and the election of Jefferson, he continued to keep an active eye on the political scene. He still wrote pamphlets, but now they accomplished less. He helped found a newspaper, the New York *Post,* to further his views and the views of his party.

But nothing could stop the decline of the Federalists. Their appeal had always been to the moneyed classes, and the moneyed classes were growing smaller in proportion to the rest of the population.

And the country was changing. New settlers were pushing west, forming new communities and demanding a greater voice in the government, leaving the more conservative easterners with less and less political power. The country was changing—becoming more "democratic"—and Hamilton knew that he and his party were losing out.

By 1801, The Grange, the house Hamilton had designed on upper Manhattan Island, was almost finished and ready for occupancy. He had gone heavily into debt to build it, but he felt that it would be a splendid place to spend what he hoped would be a peaceful and untroubled middle age, surrounded by his family.

But even while he and Eliza were moving some of their possessions into The Grange, they were struck by a personal tragedy. Again the shadow of Aaron Burr fell across Hamilton's path.

Hamilton's oldest son, Philip, nineteen years old, was attending the theater one evening late in November, 1801. In the next box sat a man named George Eacker, a Republican lawyer and a friend of Burr. Eacker made some insulting remarks about Hamilton, speaking in a loud voice so that Philip Hamilton would be sure to hear him. Outside, Philip challenged Eacker to a duel. The challenge was accepted.

Hamilton knew nothing about the duel beforehand. It was fought in New Jersey—where many duels were fought in those days—across the Hudson River from New York. Philip was wounded in the side, and was carried home to die.

Hamilton never recovered fully from his grief. It was several weeks before he was strong enough to return to his law office. Three months later he wrote to a friend, "My loss is great indeed. The brightest as well as the eldest hope of my family has been taken from me. You estimate rightly. He was a fine youth. But why should I repine? It was the will of heaven, and he is now out of reach of a world full of folly, full of vice, full of danger. . . ."

To add to Hamilton's misery, his eldest daughter, Angelica, suffered a breakdown following the shock of her brother's death. She never recovered. She became insane and remained so until her death many years later, at the age of seventy-three.

These two personal tragedies, coupled with his own political losses, drove Hamilton into a mood of deep melancholy. For a considerable time he had felt that his most important work was over, that his usefulness to his country was past. The death of Philip, the insanity of Angelica, confirmed his sense of futility. In February, 1802, he wrote a revealing letter to Gouverneur Morris, a fellow Federalist:

> Mine is an odd destiny. Perhaps no man in the United States has sacrificed or done more for the present Constitution than myself; and contrary to all my anticipations of its fate . . . I am still laboring to prop the frail and worthless fabric. Yet I have the murmurs of its friends no less than the curses of its foes for my reward. What can I do better than withdraw from the scene? Every day proves to me more and more, that this American world was not made for me.

By the end of the year, from The Grange, he could write Charles C. Pinckney, in a lighter tone but one still tinged with melancholy. "A garden, you know, is a very useful refuge [for] a disappointed politician. Accordingly, I have purchased a few acres about nine miles from town, have built a house, and am cultivating a garden. . . ."

The months passed by, with Hamilton at The Grange, a man weighed down by family sorrows and a sense of futility. And then, one day in 1804, he took up his pen and entered the political arena for the last time. The enemy?—Aaron Burr.

Since 1800, Burr's power and influence had fallen even further than Hamilton's. Jefferson did not trust Burr, feared him as a rival, and had undermined him with their party, so that by 1804, Burr knew he had no chance to win the nomination again for Vice-President.

Deeply in debt, his political future dark, Burr was a desperate man, and he decided on a desperate political scheme: he would run for Governor of New York, but he would run, not with the support of his own party, but with the support of his old political foes, the Federalists.

At the back of Burr's mind there was an even darker

scheme—secession from the Union. Several New England Federalists, violently opposed to Jefferson, hoped to lead their states out of the Union. But they dared not, unless New York were to join them. They approached Burr and offered him their support for the governorship. In return, they asked him for a promise to lead New York into secession, in a simultaneous movement with their own states.

Burr's answer was neither a firm yes, nor an absolute no. The New England Federalists were sufficiently encouraged to support Burr. They met with New York's Federalists, who agreed to back Burr for governor. All the New York Federalists, that is, except Hamilton.

It was a bitter hour for him. He had supported the Union for twenty-five years, and had done more to see its powers strengthened than any other man in America. And now the extremists in his own party were plotting to destroy the very nation which he had helped to build.

Hamilton fought Burr in that last campaign. He was the only Federalist leader to do so. And his efforts were enough. Burr was defeated by a mere five thousand votes, and the New England Federalists' dream of secession came to nothing.

During the campaign, Hamilton's private remarks were especially bitter against Burr, and several of these remarks found their way into the columns of an Albany newspaper. Burr waited two months—why he waited no one will ever know—and then he wrote to Hamilton asking whether or not those remarks had been made by him?

Hamilton's answering letter was strange. He knew that Burr hated him, that Burr was desperate, that Burr was an excellent marksman with a pistol and was clearly spoiling for a duel. Burr's letter left Hamilton an easy way out, had he chosen to take it—a way out that would in no way have compromised Hamilton's honor.

Yet in his answering letter, Hamilton wavered between two

courses; he neither admitted nor denied the remarks. His mind, which had always been so clear, so logical, so incisive, now seemed clouded with hesitation and doubt.

Burr wrote a second letter, questioning Hamilton's integrity—and now there was no escape. There was a further exchange, the duel was agreed to, and both made their secret arrangements through their seconds to meet on "the field of honor."

Why did Hamilton agree to the unnecessary duel when he had nothing to gain from it, and when he could so easily, and with honor, have avoided it? Perhaps his old political foe, John Adams, came closest to the real answer. Writing years afterwards, in 1815, Adams said, "He [Hamilton] thought he had answered the end of his creation, as far as he could see any use of his existence upon earth, and was content it should come to an end, physically or politically, if it was the pleasure of the Supreme Being."

The duel was to take place at seven in the morning on July the 11th. Two days before, Hamilton made out his will. On the 10th, he wrote the following letter to his beloved Eliza.

This letter, my dear Eliza, will not be delivered to you, unless I shall first have terminated my earthly career, to begin, as I humbly hope . . . a happy immortality. . . . I need not tell you of the pangs I feel from the idea of quitting you, and exposing you to the anguish I know you feel. . . . With my last idea I shall cherish the sweet hope of meeting you in a better world. Adieu, best of wives—best of women. Embrace all my darling children for me.

That night, retiring to his study in The Grange, Hamilton wrote a final message to Eliza. In it he explained that he had decided he would not fire at Burr.

. . . The scruples of a Christian have determined me to expose my own life to any extent, rather than subject myself to the guilt of taking the life of another. This much increases my hazards, and redoubles my pangs for you. But you had rather I should die innocent than live guilty. . . . God's will be done! The will of a merciful God must be good. Once more, adieu, my darling, darling wife.

Before the duel, Burr had spent several hours each day in target practice. On the last night he made a final settlement of his affairs. He had nothing but debts to leave to his beloved daughter, Theodosia Burr—nothing except a packet of anonymous love letters. The letters had, for the most part, been written by the wives of rich and prominent citizens, women who had been in love with Burr at some time in their lives.

Burr now supplied the names of the women, and left instructions that the letters were to be given to Theodosia on his death. With the letters he left a note, hinting that she might use them very effectively to blackmail the women who had written them. Such was the character of the Vice-President of the United States in 1804.

Early on July 11th, Hamilton set out to cross the Hudson to Weehawken, New Jersey; his second in the duel was an old friend and fellow officer, Nathaniel Pendleton. Dr. Hosack, a surgeon, accompanied them in the boat.

It was a warm morning. An early mist still hung over the silent river, and within the boat, the three men were silent too.

What Hamilton's thoughts were as the minutes passed and as the boat made its slow passage across the Hudson, no one can say exactly. But with the presence of death so near—for how could he ignore the fact that Burr hated him and that Burr was a crack shot?—what memories must have flooded back, what a curious mixture of places and events, and of long-forgotten faces suddenly recalled.

St. Croix and Peter Lytton's remote sugar plantation. His father, whom he hadn't seen in forty years. His mother, buried so long ago under the plain headstone, in the burial ground across the valley from Christiansted. The pony his father had given him—and Hugh Knox coming to their house with another set of books under his arm.

Hugh Knox, who had always said that Ham had the mark of greatness on him and who had never despaired of his future. And Nicholas Cruger, the senior partner at Cruger & Company, a man long since dead. The white rambling building that overlooked the harbor in Christiansted, the high desk where he had worked as a clerk and the quill pen he had used, and the window, with its view of the harbor and the sea—the sea that he had so often dreamed of crossing when he was a boy.

And then the terrible hurricane, and Hugh Knox sending his letter to the newspaper—and his miraculous escape to America and college.

His college friends, Ned Stevens and Robert Troup, the day in The Fields when they had suddenly boosted him up to the shaky wooden platform and he'd made a speech to the rough, excited crowd— How many speeches he had made since then, but when had he felt prouder, more gratified afterwards?

The early days of the war, at White Plains with the Hessians storming across the bridge and his cannons firing and firing again until their barrels were hot and the air was smoky. The flour mills by the Schuylkill, and the flat-bottomed boat he had steered to safety across the flooded river. "The Little Lion"—how long since anyone had called him that.

By now, he and his friend Pendleton and the doctor would have reached the middle of the Hudson, and the New Jersey shore would have begun to emerge from the mist. And the memories must have come faster now, must have tumbled out, one on the heels of the other, for the time was growing short before he met Burr.

Years before, he had ridden past that very stretch of the river, on his way north to meet General Horatio Gates, the "Hero of Saratoga." How many memories the Hudson River held for him. Not far from its upper shores he had met his future father-in-law, General Philip Schuyler, for the first time—and his future bride, Eliza. At Poughkeepsie, where the Hudson was wider and more majestic, he had fought his battle against Governor Clinton and the Anti-Federalists. He had fought so many battles for his adopted country, as a soldier, as a pamphleteer, as a politician, as the first Secretary of the Treasury—but to what purpose? The country had no use for his talents now, and no love for his ideas.

And as the boat glided up to the New Jersey shore, his mind must have grown dark as he thought of all his wasted efforts—for without any doubt he believed that those efforts had been wasted.

He was unable to foresee the future of the country that he had done so much to create. He believed that the Union would soon be dissolved, that the Constitution would be torn to shreds, and that the States would become weak, separate little countries, forever incapable of courageous or noble actions. And so he was convinced of the futility of much of his life, and was unaware of the debt the United States would owe to his memory.

At Weehawken, Hamilton and his party found Burr and his second at the prearranged spot, an open circle of ground within a thick grove of trees.

Hamilton and Burr nodded. Their seconds brought out the pistols. Hamilton and Burr took their positions.

Pendleton stepped back. There was a moment's silence, broken only by the rustle of the leaves. Then Pendleton gave the word. Burr raised his arm, aimed, fired. Hamilton rose, turned sideways, and as he fell forward, his pistol fired high into the trees.

Burr and his second left as Dr. Hosack hurried up to Hamilton. "This is a mortal wound," Hamilton said. Then he fainted.

The doctor examined the wound, and said that the pistol ball had found a vital spot in Hamilton's side. He and Pendleton carried the dying Hamilton back to the boat.

Before they had reached the New York shore, Hamilton regained consciousness. "My vision is indistinct," he said. Then his eye fell on the case with the dueling pistols. "Take care of that pistol," he said, not realizing that he had fired involuntarily. "It is still cocked. Pendleton knows that I did not intend to fire at him."

They carried Hamilton to the house of a friend, William Bayard, on Jane Street, and sent a message to Eliza at The Grange.

Sedatives were given to the dying man, but his agony was indescribable. For thirty-one hours he lay in Bayard's house, before death finally came at two in the afternoon.

At the news of Hamilton's death, there was a great shift in public feeling. A few days before, Hamilton had merely been a prominent New York lawyer, and the leader of an almost extinct political party. Overnight a forgetful populace remembered. He became a hero again.

The city went into mourning, and as the news spread, the entire nation followed. His services to his adopted country were now recalled; his career as a soldier on Washington's staff, his fight for the Constitution; his *Federalist* papers; his achievements as the first Secretary of the Treasury. When it was learned that he had died deeply in debt, a fund was raised in New York to aid his widow and children.

A tremendous funeral parade was held to honor his memory. The flag-draped coffin carried his body through the city's narrow streets to the churchyard of Trinity Church, at the foot of Wall Street, where he was buried with full military honors.

His tombstone may be seen in Trinity churchyard today, its letters eroded by wind and rain. The inscription on the headstone bears these words:

TO THE MEMORY OF
ALEXANDER HAMILTON
THE CORPORATION OF TRINITY HAVE ERECTED THIS
MONUMENT
IN TESTIMONY OF THEIR RESPECT
FOR
THE PATRIOT OF INCORRUPTIBLE INTEGRITY
THE SOLDIER OF APPROVED VALOR
THE STATESMAN OF CONSUMMATE WISDOM
WHOSE TALENTS AND VIRTUES WILL BE ADMIRED
BY
GRATEFUL POSTERITY
LONG AFTER THIS MARBLE SHALL HAVE MOULDERED TO
DUST
HE DIED JULY 12TH, 1804, AGED 47

BIBLIOGRAPHY

Atherton, Gertrude, Editor, *A Few of Hamilton's Letters*. The Macmillan Company, New York, 1903.

Atherton, Gertrude, *The Conqueror*. J. B. Lippincott Co., Philadelphia, 1943.

Autobiography of Thomas Jefferson. G. P. Putnam's Sons, New York, 1959.

Bowen, Catherine Drinker, *John Adams and the American Revolution*. (Atlantic Monthly Press) Little Brown, Boston 1950.

Chesterton, Cecil, *A History of the United States*. E. P. Dutton Company, Inc., New York.

Hacker, Louis M., *Alexander Hamilton in the American Tradition*. McGraw-Hill Book Co., Inc., New York, 1957.

Miller, William, *A History of the United States*. Dell Publishing Co., Inc., New York.

Morris, Richard B., Editor, *The Basic Ideas of Alexander Hamilton*. Pocket Books, Inc., New York.

Nye, R. B. and Morpurgo, J. E., *A History of the United States*. Penguin Books, Inc., Baltimore.

Schachner, Nathan, *Alexander Hamilton*. Thomas Yoseloff, Inc., New York, 1957.

INDEX

THE AUTHOR

William Wise is a versatile writer. His work for adults has appeared in such magazines as the *Virginia Quarterly Review, Saturday Review, Yale Review,* etc. He has also written a volume of children's verse, several teen-age biographies and two picture books. Mr. Wise is a full-time writer who has lived in New York City all his life.

speeches, he was an outspoken advocate or strong federal government. As the recognize leader of the Federalist party, he laid th groundwork for the Constitutional Conver tion in 1787 and then successfully led th fight for ratification of the Constitution b the states of the new nation.

When he was Secretary of the Treasury, on of Hamilton's many far-reaching proposals t solve the country's grave financial difficultie was the creation of a national bank. Thoug his policies were finally put into effect — an were to assure the country a stable econom for years to come — their originator wa strongly opposed by Thomas Jefferson, whos rivalry with Hamilton was surpassed only b that of Hamilton's most bitter enemy and h final opponent—Aaron Burr.

Here is an absorbingly related story of th personal and political achievements, as we as the frustrations and rivalries that marke the life of a brilliant and controversial Amer ican statesman.